LIES,
CRIMINALS
AND
BULLDUST

LINDA PARKER

LINDA PARKER

Dedicated to
Robyn and Rhonda,
who took this journey with me.

First printing 2021

ISBN 978-0-9945133-7-3

FORWARD

This is the story of my life up till the age of eleven. I have endeavoured to be as close to the facts as is possible. The stories and memories I have of childhood may vary to that of others, but I see the world through my eyes and the position I hold in my family. These are my feelings and experiences of growing up. I have changed the names of many of the characters but have decided to leave others.

Through the freedom of information, I was able to obtain small snippets of my time in care and what lead to that. Sometimes the paperwork only held an entry of one or two lines, but it became extremely important in helping me place the timeline. The information, although confronting, gave me insight into the legal and welfare systems of the time. I spent many months waiting in anticipation for my information which I obtained from a great organisation called Open Place.

I too am a forgotten Australian, and it might surprise you that I am a white Caucasian.

My father's stories, repeated over many years, were sketchy around the edges (the bits he always left out) so I opted to fill in the gaps as best as I could. Not living most of my life with him, I suppose I never got right to the edges.

There were also pieces of my mother's stories that she left out. Sometimes the truth is hard to face and fear of judgment is reason to remove the detail. I have not written my story to purposely hurt or demoralise anyone. I have real love in my heart for my parents and the circumstances that they found themselves in.

I tell my story for all those who sit in judgement of others. We are not all born into happy households. Some of us have had to swim our way through massive tidal surges to be able to breathe. And now I stand on the beach and watch that water disperse and disappear. It holds no fear now. I am victorious.

I AM ME

My hatred of the cold has manifested from my time spent in the highlands of Seymour. A time when I could feel the pain of misery that only comes when you are fighting for survival. Even now that I am old, I am reminded of the winter cold. And I cringe and I whine at the pain I feel at its arrival.

And when summer comes, I celebrate its warmth at the ocean. A place that holds my happiness, my magic, and my freedom. As I walk its shores or swim its waters, it is the sounds of the waves that instantly calms my soul.

I have been here before. In those snippets of childhood that were lull, I could just be a child.

In history there were whole civilisations of people that worshiped the sun gods. Maybe my Karma (my memory) is rooted way back in those societies.

The sun, with its every blinking eye of light and warmth, shone for me even through my darkest days. And although it was sometimes shadowed or clouded from view, I knew it was there.

It is only now that I understand my being. I am a product of memory. All of us are unique with our memories of life. But the sun is my god. For when it shines so, too, do I.

Cobwebs in the cupboard is a metaphor of secrets locked away from the light. My family's belief is that theirs could lie here and die in the darkness.

But not so. For I have opened that door and dusted that web. Its danger lies in the vermin left stuck to its fibre.

But the web is destroyed now, and its power is gone. My mother's family were not just a product of their time, but a product of ignorance, cruelty and violence. Their struggle was not just that of poverty, but of mental health as well.

Without adequate support and understanding of human suffering, many were never diagnosed until much later, creating an impossible amount of heartache and wretchedness for not just their generation, but for subsequent ones.

My stubbornness and independence come from sheer survival. I gritted my teeth and pushed through all the challenges encountered in life. My courage and determination remained hidden from most as I chose my paths through time. Who was interested in my plight, anyhow? No-one, I believe. Only me. And it is me that continues to find my place in the world.

But I'm grateful for many things. And I continue to find the good in the now and not in the past.

I hope this story makes you aware of the hardships many people face when they are born and raised in disharmonious families. As a child I had no choice but to watch the self-destruction going on all around me. But I am not to blame. I may have taken a million steps along my journey of life, but it is the ones I am taking today that matter most.

PART ONE:

BIRTHS, DEATHS AND MARRIAGE

MAY STARTS SCHOOL, 1946

May had problems. Her childhood had been taken and her parents failed to protect her. She grew unhappy and withdrawn. Children are compelled to live the life they were given, and May's would break her. When little May started school, she was expected to ride a bike. Only thing was she hadn't learnt to pedal properly yet. So Antoinette, in her wisdom, decided to tie her daughter's feet to the pedals, and push her off at the gate. 'Boys! Make sure she keeps pedalling, and doesn't stop until she reaches the school,' their mother called after them.

May tried to pedal fast and block the fear of falling out of her mind. The bike was high. And her brothers fast. She had to stretch her legs long to keep the wheels turning.

'Hurry up, May! We'll be late,' the boys called, looking back to check how far behind their sibling was.

The not-heavily-used road was more like a track made for locals to access the main road from their properties. Her calf muscles ached and the seat uncomfortable between her legs. The gravel made a lovely scrunching sound as her bike wheels rolled over the stone particles. Trying to concentrate on the sound helped distract her from the burning in her legs. She rode on.

Was that a Kookaburra laughing, daring her to fall? There were plenty of birds in the bush. Maybe one of those noisy cockatoos who had learnt how to laugh. Or was it all in her mind. Her mind bothered her sometimes, especially when she had to listen to her parents arguing and yelling. Couldn't they see that it scared her? She loved the wild birds in the bush. They brightened her life with song, not arguments.

May called out to her brothers up ahead, 'Please wait. I'm going as fast as I can.'

Turning, they looked in her direction. Her brothers both loved her and were protective towards her. She knew they had not meant to leave her behind but were keen to arrive in time to play before the bell.

May got nearer to her brothers. Trying to clear her mind of the surroundings, she focused instead on them.

She steered the handlebars slightly to the right but lost her point of gravity. The bike wobbled uncontrollably. In a desperate attempt to avoid crashing into the boys, May applied the pedal brake, hard. Skidding in the dirt, the bike toppled over. Still moving, it managed to drag her trapped body along the gravel underneath it. She screamed in agony as the stones shredded her skin.

The boys had watched her fall and ran to her aid. Tears streamed down her cheeks, her wails lasting long enough to take her breath. It hurt bad. Trying to stay calm, she concentrated on their soft words and offers of help. Together they attempted to stand the bike. Realising this was too difficult, her brothers decided to untie her feet with the frame still on the ground. 'Stay still and try to stop crying. We'll have you untied quicker if you stop.'

May's howling had been replaced with sobs, and the tears kept flowing freely. Her face a mess, stained with tears and gravel dust. *I must be brave.* She bit her bottom lip. It was hard, real hard.

Especially when all she was aware of, was the blood trickling from her knees. Oh dear, she didn't dare look, because blood made her dizzy.

When finally, they managed to free her and help her stand, Donald gasped in disbelief. "Oh shit!

Look at her knees.'

Frank looked green around the gills as he wrapped his arm around his sister.

'Let's leave our bikes in the grass and pick them up on the way home,' Donald suggested.

And off they all walked down the road.

My grandmother got a beating for that episode. And my mother never forgot her first day of school.

**

MAY'S HOME IN THE VALLEY

May's two older brothers treasured her. And when she was born, her mother Antionette was elated to finally have a healthy baby girl.

Times when they were alone, May's mother had told her the heart rendering story of her twin sisters. Without all the intimate details of course, as it wouldn't be right for May to hear. But she knew the facts. And the horrible secret always spoken about in times of anger. And there were moments when her mother cried from the sadness of it all. But it was all secret talk from days past.

Her father never spoke of it. And May would not speak to him about such matters, for fear of punishment. She was terrified of him, but she knew his involvement. May knew the truth.

Only small in stature, her father was a weedy looking man and not someone you would instantly be fearful of. In fact, to others he didn't really appear to be the type to bully his family.

May often whined to her mother, in the hope that she would somehow be allowed to drive into town with her parents. But usually they picked the eldest son Donald as his strength and agility was more useful than her chattering.

So mostly she stayed at home. Only leaving when she was allowed to attend school a few miles up the road. She lived

9

where the bush met the valley, and the wildlife grazed on its pastures. Where the native birds watching her distress from the tops of the trees were her friends, cawing and shrieking (she was sure) to warn someone of her plight.

Rolling hills in the distant landscape lay like renaissance models. But she never really felt their beauty. Her world was not soft and pretty and full of art but harsh and ugly and full of never-ending-work. Here in the valley, she was trapped in her world. Forty-Five miles from town.

A gentleman in public, her father was good at concealment. But if you looked closely into his eyes, his falsehood mirrored what lurked inside. His eyes were the windows to his deranged and misguided mind. May refused to look into them. They frightened her so.

'Antoinette!' he shouted one day. 'Get May to bring me some lunch later this morning. It is very hard work carving out the bush. I will need a substantial meal.'

May, standing nearby, hung her head and looked to the ground. Dare she try and complain? Her mind raced and she was at risk at wetting herself. She decided she would, even though she knew there would be a scolding to follow. 'Not me, I don't want to go! Please let the boys go. I don't want to!'

Antionette nodded. 'It won't take them long and they will be quicker than May. Besides there are bloody snakes down there! She's too little to be walking the bush alone.'

Her father instantly fired up, raising his voice. 'The boys are busy, do you hear me? They have their jobs to do. And you' —he pointed a finger at May— 'will do what you're told!' He turned to his wife, his eyes glittering. 'And you will see she does it, Antoinette.'

May could feel his eyes drilling into her. She couldn't look up. It somehow gave him more power. she concentrated on rubbing her bare foot backwards and forwards in the dirt, watching it fluff up fine dust and leaving lovely smooth patches of compacted earth.

'Do you hear me? Do you? Look at me!'

May turned her eyes upwards, to where his lips held his bitter words.

'There'll be a trouble if you do not obey me.'

She watched him mouth it. And knew he meant it. She'd felt his wrath before.

May wanted to cry. But she knew he'd start raging at her. So, she nodded yes. And he won. Again.

May knew her real name. She could spell it because it was written on the little cross that she would visit whenever she wanted to talk to her baby sisters. It was her place of comfort, whenever her mother would run away into the bush. Sometimes it was days before she would return. May knew her body would be blackened, it always was, but she dared not look.

She would whisper to her angels, but they would not whisper back. She did not want him to hear because he would be angry. Had he killed her this time? Would he one day bury her mother, here beside her angels? And would she then be compelled to visit two crosses instead of one?

Thankfully her mother always returned. May was given four more sisters to love. Lilly was born after May. Her hair was dark when everyone else was blonde. Lilly was her favourite, and they were the best of friends. She was always busy now with so many chores to do. Helping with Virginia, Alina, and Bonnie meant she no longer spent as much time pondering the tiny grave. But there was comfort in knowing they were there. And one day she would meet both of them in Heaven. And smother them with kisses.

When her father was finally caught for all his criminal behaviour, he was taken to jail. The authorities rushed him away, and his reign of terror on her and her family ended. Traumatic and disruptive turmoil followed, but May was glad to be free of him. He could no longer wield his power over her. He was gone and she felt safe. But it didn't last. Now in her teens, May would wrestle with her mind. Years of abuse crashing into her psyche, a wave of emotion of guilt and madness and sheer depression.

Her family's decision to move from their maternal home in the central west, to Deniliquin in the south, saw them leave behind her loved eldest brother, Donald. His decision to stay and tend and toil the valley was heart-wrenching. Everyone cried. No one more than him.

The gum trees would now stand guard over the grave of her sisters. And the poplar trees would whisper the sins of the past. And May would try to pick up the pieces of her life in a new place and start again.

***

LEAVING THE VALLEY

May had been residing with a family in town since the arrest of her father, and moving to the Riverina town of Deniliquin meant she could return to join her family.

May's Uncle Otto had set up his car repair workshop in the North of Deni, and was keen to help them move closer to him and his brood. Otto was a good man. He had told May's mother that he was upset about the recent goings on and could not stand by and watch his sister and her children suffer any more. 'You must escape while he is gone. May is still a young teen and can start a new life away from here,' he said. 'I will offer you my support.'

So, they set about packing their belongings. Deciding what to take and what to leave behind became their constant conversation.

They could take their time and when her family was ready, Uncle Otto arrived one day to transport the family from their valley home.

The weather that morning was stifling. The air so still, you could nearly hear the grasshoppers chewing in the paddocks.

All May's bush birds were sleeping. Or perhaps they were hiding in the shade, away from the heat of the morning. Either way, none of them were there to watch her leave. How she would miss their beautiful song. And the way they called to her whenever she'd stroll past their overhead perches.

May took her last look around. She no longer felt she belonged here. As if she'd stepped out into the world already. Out of this picture and into a new one— a better one.

She ran to the grave of her sisters and whispered her goodbyes. Knowing she may never be back, tore at her heart. But they were not here anyhow, because she knew they were with Jesus. And Jesus was with God. And that's all she needed to know.

May turned her attention to her brother Donald, running over to join the group of family members crammed around the caravan of goods, that were hooked to the end, and loaded on the back of her Uncle's truck. He had decided to stay in the valley and tend to the farm. He was the eldest after all and very capable. Besides, he told her someone needs to be here when father returned.

It was time to leave and their chattering had been replaced with wishes and kisses of goodbye. Her brother tried to be heroic, but barely kept it together. May took her turn, wrapped her arms around him, and sobbed. 'I'm gonna miss you. Write to me. And don't forget, we all love you.'

He muttered something about being all right and that he'd miss her too. It was too painful to really take in, so she let it wash over her.

Turning away, she jumped up into the back of the vehicle, squeezing in between Lilly and Virginia.

As she watched, Donald moved back towards the house. The realisation that he would be all alone without them weighed heavily on her conscience.

Was she to blame for this sordid mess? No, her father was the one to blame. Hadn't he been taken to jail? Her family, however, were now fatherless, homeless, fractured, and destitute.

Otto was a nice man and insisted her family stay with him and his wife Stella and their children.

May and her family made the best of it. But with ten children and three adults in the house, it was often noisy and there was nowhere to escape from each other. May was used to open spaces with bush and native animals, not the confines of a fringe suburban block. It took a lot of adjusting.

And with the adults constantly discussing the family's misfortune, she felt shamed and responsible.

Her only reprieve were the school hours, when she could just enjoy her studies of History or Maths. Or just talk to her school friends about teen things. And be ordinary like the rest of the class.

But when the school bell rang, she knew she would take the bus back to that cramped house on the North Side with her cousins, and her young siblings, and all the mayhem that went with it.

Oh, she would surely go mad if she had to live like this for much longer.

**

A NEW LIFE BY THE RIVER

With the conjoining of the two families, it wasn't long before things began to unravel and other alternatives were sought.

Her mother Antoinette, with help from Otto, purchased a parcel of land by the Edward River. And together they made plans to establish a new farm. One that would be able to sustain the family.

May found it a really nice spot. She no longer felt the isolation she had when she had lived in the Valley.

This property was only five miles from town and not too far to ride if she needed to shop. Its farm gate was situated on a busy main road and the neighbours were relatively close.

Lovely Australian River Red Gums trailed the river's bank, soaking their roots in the shallow edges of the water. And clusters of introduced European Weeping Willows, their lovely canes swaying like islanders in grass skirts whenever the wind blew.

However, the River was not crystal clear and coloured blue, but instead a murky brown silt, and its banks a grey powdery dust. This made it hard to spot the water snakes that swam past in the current. The abundance of tree debris, gum leaves and broken limbs floating in patches here and there made snake camouflage possible too.

May hated them. She was scared of snakes. But she was *really terrified* of earth worms. As far back as she could remember, her brothers had chased her with those vile slithering Annelids. She'd developed a phobia.

They would dangle them up in front of her face, just so she could really get a good look at their revolting features. And then they'd torture her by forcefully trying to stuff them into her clothing.

It usually ended badly, with her running around trying to get them out, screeching uncontrollably.

They forced her fingers to touch their cool soft rubbery skins. Their ends like a blunt crayon. And their bodies with rings of coiled flesh.

She particularly hated the way they would move their worm snouts around, as if they were sniffing something. Blind without an eye to be seen. She was sure they were alien. Their smell of earth and mud made her dry retch. She didn't like thinking about them, ever.

Her brothers would by now, be rolling around belly laughing at her. She hated them when they did this.

***

HARVEY

Where did Harvey come from? May wasn't sure. Someone Uncle Otto knew perhaps? A fishing friend? A customer from his workshop? Somehow, he appeared one day just like magic.

It seemed like her mother Antoinette knew him well. Had she been keeping him a secret for a while? May was not sure. But now he was hanging around and joining her family by the river.

May couldn't believe it. She didn't want a strange male shacking up with them and ordering her around. Her family were just getting settled and learning to fend for themselves. She didn't miss having her father around with all that violence and abuse. She just wished Harvey would go away.

A woman on her own often attracted men who wanted to do the chivalrous thing. But there were other things that attracted a man to a woman, and May was sure that this was also his intent.

It soon became apparent that Harvey didn't want to go away. Unfortunately. Instead he invited himself along, whether May liked it or not!

Harvey excelled at building and expertly dug endless dirt for the veggie gardens. So, he had his uses. And that meant her mother was keen to keep him, even if she wasn't.

May was happy that Harvey shared the workload, as it meant less work for her to do.

'We don't like him either,' May's sisters told her. 'We know mother needs a strong man to help with the manual work, as it's difficult when you're a woman. But he is always growling and standing over us, making our lives unbearable. And whenever we speak to Mother about this, she doesn't listen to us. Not even if we persist. She always sides with him.'

Her sisters were always plotting his goodbyes or hoping he might one day drown in the river. May and her sisters realised very early on that their mother had swapped their tyrant father for a tyrant stranger. There was in fact nothing that any of them could do to get rid of him.

May watched ecstatically the progress of a small two-roomed cottage being built out on the property. And they spent the weekends out by the muddy river carving out their new life.

Harvey added a small lean-to tacked on the side to reside in away from the family.

May liked that he was separated from them. She thought it best that he kept to himself, then she didn't have to interact with him too much. Men scared her and she had no trust in their intention, so it was easier to just keep out of his way.

The house was built straight on the ground. May helped her mother lay hessian bags from the stock feed. And Uncle Otto had given them a couple of second-hand rugs. That would certainly help keep the dust down and make it home-like.

They decked out one room with a mishmash of beds to sleep in. The littlest ones usually bunked together, and Antoinette often spent the night in Harvey's lean-to.

The other room contained the crammed kitchen, and not all of them could sit at the table together in one sitting. May didn't care about that too much. It was just good to finally have somewhere to call home.

May helped in the garden, digging the sandy soil and planting the many seeds they had brought with them from the Valley.

Having no infrastructure made it very difficult as all the newly planted veggies had to be watered by hand. And it was May's job to carry the water from the river in metal buckets to soak everything.

Sometimes she managed to encourage her tween siblings to help her with the task, which made the workload a little easier.

Her relentless trips to the river became exhausting. It seemed every soaking of water she applied to the garden was swallowed up within seconds of pouring. Her constant cartage all day until nightfall made her hands blister and her body ache from fatigue.

She didn't complain, however, as Frank and her mother busily built the enclosures to house the newly acquired poultry, so they could have eggs and meat to eat. Even her school-aged sisters were expected to spend endless hours caring for Alina and Bonnie after they arrived home every day after their studies.

As the weather intensified and the veggie patch grew, we adapted other ways to help with its constant watering. We installed concrete tanks and Frank set up a pump to siphon water from the river.

Virginia, Lilly and Alina enjoyed gathering the newly laid eggs from the chickens and ducks, so they were allotted the job of feeding and filling the water containers in the poultry cages. May happily passed on the monotonous chore of cleaning and filling their drinking vessels.

***

JAILBIRDS

May started school with her brother and younger siblings on her arrival in Deniliquin. But she abandoned her education when she and her younger sisters were teased and bullied while riding their bikes home one afternoon.

On that day, a group of boys followed them along the river bridge that crossed to the North of the town. They called to the girls.

May chatted to Lilly about the chores that had to be done when they arrived home, so didn't really hear what the boys had said and chose to ignore them. She pedalled slowly and steadily. She didn't see the need to hurry, as Virginia was lagging behind a little and needed to catch up. May turned her head and observed Virginia's position at the back of Lilly's wheel. 'All good.' She smiled at Lilly.

May had to watch Virginia, as she was still quite young. Otherwise Mother would belt her. "You are older, May," her mother's voice echoed in her ears. "You are responsible for getting them home from school safely."

May called out, 'Come on Virginia, Alina will be waiting to play when you get home.'

'Hey, you jailbirds! You listening to us?' an aggressive male voice called from somewhere behind them.

At first, May hadn't realised that the boys were referring to her and her sisters.

'Hey jailbirds!' they taunted again. 'Heard your father's in the cells.'

'Arr stop, you're killing me.' His smart-arse friend sniggered, smiling at his mates for approval.

May couldn't believe it. Were they really talking to her? And if so, why were they being so cruel.

She had not told anyone of their family's shame. She tried to concentrate. What should she do? *Maybe they meant to hurt her and her sisters.* Her mind clouded in a haze of emotion, swirling like a ghostly fog and taking her back to the valley and all its nightmares. She could hear her father's breathing as he violated her. The sounds of bush and the smell of fear. Yes. She could smell the fear.

Her heart raced and her hands turned clammy on the handlebars. She feared falling off her bike and took deep breaths to calm herself. It was a real struggle to concentrate and brush aside their taunts.

'Hurry!' May yelled to Virginia and Lilly. 'Pedal faster.' Her adrenaline kicked in as her fight-flight instinct rose to the surface, and she took off at top speed. She should look back but was too charged with hormone to slow the survival mode. She hoped like hell her sisters were able to keep up.

Gasping, and coughing, she could barely breathe. Not just from the exertion, but from sheer panic and terror. The memory of her father flooding back was too much.

Lilly pedalled up from behind, shouting out to May. 'Wait for us! May, please wait.'

May turned to see her sisters pedalling like crazy in single file.

Poor little Virginia was welling up ready to burst into tears and whining about how hard it was to ride fast.

Lilly, tall, with an athletic build, had very little trouble in sprinting off and putting distance between her, and the perpetrators. But poor Virginia struggled with her old bike. Hers was a hand-me-down rust bucket with a seat that wobbled and pedals that were stiff and hard to push.

'Jailbirds. Jailbirds,' they chanted. 'Your father's in the cells.'

The boys skidded to a stop and jumped from their bikes. Picking up handfuls of pebbles, they began throwing stones at May and her sisters. As the pebbles rained against their wheels and whizzed past their heads, they continued on.

Manual work had made them all fit and strong, so they pedalled with gusto and out-cycled the group of bullies.

However, the boys were relentless in the pursuit of the girls. They jumped back on their bicycles and chased them nearly half the way home.

How had they found out about such private matters? It was terribly upsetting, and May couldn't stop crying for the rest of the way home, making it very difficult to see the road through watery lenses.

Life was so cruel, and she wondered if people would ever leave her alone and let her forget about her past.

'Are you all right?' her sisters said together.

'I'm just fine,' she answered (when really, she wasn't). 'I don't want to talk about it. Come on you two. We're nearly home.'

***

MAY LEAVES SCHOOL

May lasted a little while longer at school, but she was never really happy attending anymore. Eventually Antoinette decided that May would spend her days on the farm and work instead of wasting time with study.

Her workload was monotonous and tiring, and her refusal to kill any of the animals on the property didn't please her mother. Harvey and Antoinette had taken to murdering chickens, ducks and the recently acquired turkeys for an income source. It distressed May and she wanted no part of it.

Having to stand and watch as her mother broke their necks disgusted her. As for plucking all their feathers and pulling guts and giblets from their poor carcasses no, she wasn't going to do such a barbaric thing.

Her mother became frustrated and angry at her for refusing to help with the execution of the poultry. May hated that Antoinette bullied and yelled at her. Sometimes her mother would spit out her frustration, telling May how hard she had to work and how her life was ruined. 'It is your fault.' She would snarl at her.

And May would slink off and think her mother was right, maybe it was her fault that her family were struggling to survive.

May really hated herself for being weak and stupid. She decided to work hard and show her mother that she was worthy of love.

Maybe it was her fault that her mother wanted to end her own life. May wasn't sure exactly what was in that little brown bottle, but she'd been told its contents held a poison capable of killing.

May began to feel like the world around her might just swallow her. Why did her head hurt? And why did it feel like the voice in it was always trying to make her feel bad? Were there two of her? She didn't feel loved. And she certainly didn't feel appreciated. At times it was lonely in her head. And frightening. Yes, sometimes it was frightening.

She couldn't complain or talk to her mother about her feelings; Antoinette would be too busy or not interested. Harvey took up a lot of her time and he certainly didn't want to hear what she had to say.

May kept her feelings to herself. It was easier. Here in Deniliquin there was no father to abuse her. But her mother's reminder of the incest, was nearly as harmful. May could not forget, or heal the guilt that she held in her heart.

Sometimes when her sisters were asleep beside her, she would lie awake and think about ending it all. Only she wouldn't flaunt it like her mother, no she would just do it. It would be quite easy really with the Edward River not far from the house. It was very deep in the middle, and she could not swim well. It certainly wouldn't take long.

If she entered the water when the current was strong it would carry her down-stream. That way she wouldn't have to die in front of her family. And by the time they realised she had disappeared it would be too late. She would have drowned, and the snakes would be slithering away from her, having realised she was too big to eat.

They could bury her in the ground. And she could have a white cross with her real name etched into it. Only then could she finally meet her little sister angels.

Her mind was a constant bother. Within it, were her swirling bad thoughts and dark images. She wondered would she ever be free of turmoil. Depression followed her like a shadow, forever threatening to black her out into a silhouette.

May watched as the farm slowly started to take shape and become more orderly. When the rain tanks were built and the irrigation from the river siphoned, the situation improved for everyone.

Alina and Bonnie were too young to attend school, and spent their days playing near May. They loved to watch her work and followed her around, only abandoning her when the other girls arrived home in the afternoon.

May's responsibilities continued to grow. Cramming in more and more chores as the need arose, she was always exhausted by the end of the day. But at least it was a distraction from her mind filled with doom.

At least, Lilly and Virginia had the responsibility of the young ones after school. It was hard work making sure they never wandered down to the river. Or got into any mischief around the place.

And those two girls often put the dinner on and fed all the little ones before May even finished her day. She marvelled at their skill and patience.

Many fruit trees dotted the farm, and Antoinette bought a cow to hand milk, using the thick cream she scooped off the top to churn into butter. The coops that their brother Frank had helped to build were now bursting with feathered birds.

Very soon they were not only growing food for themselves, but May and her sisters were selling the excess to the traffic that passed by their farm gate.

May set up a produce barrow, wheeling the contents of vegetables, fruit, eggs and flower bulbs up and down the gravel entrance to the road. She spent hours stocking and selling their wares. Not even in the heat of summer or the frosts of winter did she stop working.

Frank had started working for an earthmoving company. His wages certainly helped, and he was expected to forfeit a great portion of it. Everyone had to contribute what they could.

After three years of farm labour at home, May got a job.

***

A NEW JOB

May's neighbours, the Kendals needed someone to help clean their magnificent homestead. After asking her mother, it was agreed that she could start work as soon as possible. Excitement filled May as she could now work inside instead of trudging around in the elements.

The Kendal homestead sat beside the Edward River like May's house, but the comparison stopped there.

Unlike them, the Kendals lived in a splendid home of timber floorboards and window frames.

Views of distant landscapes framed in carved wood decorated their sitting room. Curtains and soft furnishings of the finest fabrics draped the glass panes and couches. May loved the sitting room in all its stately glory. Cleaning in here did not classify as a chore but simply sheer delight.

In the dining room, portraits of family members with handsome faces looked down at May from the walls, as she dusted all the trinkets of metal and porcelain.

This splendid family home delighted May. The Kendals were as refined as her family were not. Smart business people made their fortune from wool and rice. Generations of hard work and smart choices displayed in their assets.

It was easier here for her. Her mind would calm as she would go about her work. Her employers were fair and kind, never pushing her to do more. They trusted her to complete her tasks as she could.

May often worked at the Kendal's until late afternoon, so she had some freedom from the drudgery of her farm life and the torment of her mother.

***

THE DANCE

May's job at the Kendal's meant she could afford a few small luxury items. A lipstick, a new pair of shoes and a few yards of material.

She gave her mother most of her earnings but could keep a little for herself.

There was a dance to be held in Echuca and May intended to go. She gained permission from her mother, and Uncle Otto would chaperone her to the event. Excitement coursed through her, and she worked even harder, so she could save for a handbag and compact to complete her look.

Her mother helped out by sewing a new dress for the occasion. A lovely swing frock of pink tulle, with a fitted bodice of printed pink floral.

The material highlighted her blonde hair and magically made her blue eyes sparkle. Perhaps the addition of a little makeup she'd applied for the first time and her new pink lipstick also helped. Whatever it was, she was very happy with the results. And excitedly waited for Otto to arrive.

May felt like Cinderella as she waited for her transport. All her days of hard work were now paying off. She was finally allowed one night off to attend the Ball. And Otto, yes kind Uncle Otto would be her Footman.

May, just like the story of Cinderella, was on a time limit. 'You must be home by eleven. Or else there will be trouble. Make sure you don't keep Otto waiting.'

May rolled her eyes. 'I won't.'

'Have a good time.'

'I will,' May called back as she headed out the door to the sound of Otto's car pulling up in the drive. 'Bye.'

She climbed in beside her cousin Winnie, who was also attending the function, and Otto drove off out the drive and onto the highway towards town.

May and Winnie had a lovely evening at the Hall. Learning dance steps and chatting with each other. There were other girls she knew from Deniliquin here, so May soon relaxed and began to enjoy herself.

The band played a good mix of old and new tunes. The ones she knew, she sang along to with the rest of the crowd.

May loved music. It was the only thing that made her feel happy. Music seemed to soften the edges of her hard life a little.

During the night some of the young men were actually interested in dancing with her. She had never felt so giddy with pleasure before. She really wasn't looking to hitch up with anyone. It was just so much fun to dance and flirt.

However, she wished the one named Cyril would just give up and leave her alone. He really wasn't her type. His persistence to dance was starting to bug her. She had already danced a couple of slow ones with him, and he got a little fresh.

Whenever the band stopped for a breather, he tried to get her outside. She didn't know him at all and thought it best to stay inside. Besides Uncle Otto was around somewhere and she didn't want to get caught in a precarious situation. Not that she was interested in Cyril.

She much preferred some of the other young men she had danced with over the course of the evening and decided to ignore him and dance with some of the others instead.

Way too soon it was time to leave, and Otto rounded them up and ushered Winnie and her out of the Hall, and into the car for the return journey.

As they headed out of town, the traffic was bumper to bumper on the Cobb Highway.

It seemed to her that half of Deniliquin had attended the Echuca Ball tonight.

Talking to Otto about her night of fun helped to take the focus off the doom looming just under the surface of her subconscious.

Winnie was on a high too and hummed some of the tunes trying to calm her. Earlier in the evening, May had voiced her fears to Winnie about her need to be home on time. Her cousin knew all too well how May's family conducted themselves. *Bless her. She was a good person.*

Uncle Otto chatted happily unperturbed about her lateness. But May could not relax, and anxiety built up in her mind at the thought of the lecture she would receive on her arrival home.

If only the traffic would speed up a little.

Once at May's home, Otto didn't stop and speak to Antoinette. Instead he waved May goodbye and departed instantly. As she watched his car lights disappear, she stood in the dark contemplating her excuse, when the door burst open and her mother instructed her to come inside.

May knew as soon as she entered the room that it was not going to be good. It was as if the air held the tension and the walls trapped the demons of evil in their paintwork.

Harvey started to beat her. Lashing his temper at her with raised voice and cursed words.

May tried to explain the traffic situation, but he shut her down with a strike to her face.

Where is mother? She scoured the dull room. *Mother will tell him it's okay. The traffic held them up.*

May continued her defence, swearing she had done nothing wrong.

But he continued his onslaught.

Her mother watched in the shadows like an accomplice.

'Stop him!' May's eyes found her mother's. 'What are you doing?' she screamed at Antoinette.

But her mother just stood there and said nothing, as Harvey continued his assault.

'You are a tramp! A whore! Where have you been?' he bellowed, striking her again with a backhander.

Her head reeled as she stumbled back and slid down the wall, her arms placed in front of her face as she cowered, curled in a ball, with her knees up. She grabbed her arms together in an attempt to shield herself from anymore strikes to her head.

'Get up!' His voice boomed like thunder.

She rolled away from where he stood, towering over her, and got to her feet. She tasted blood as she wiped the back of her hand across her swollen lips. She must have sustained some pretty bad injuries.

May stumbled, almost falling out the door and into the darkness. The fresh night air filled her lungs and started bringing her back to life. She ran. She ran full of anger and hatred and determination. She would not forgive them.

The moon shone a little, but it wasn't enough to light her way. It would have to be guesswork. She had come this way along the river before and tonight the thought of snakes didn't bother her. Snakes were not as frightening as *him*. He might have killed her if she hadn't scrambled out the door. And what for? She had done nothing.

If she followed the river, she could reach the Kendal's homestead. And if she could see where the path to their house was in the dark, she could get help. Surely they would take pity on her.

He'd beaten her badly. She doubled over in pain from the stitch caused by running as well as from the punches he had fired at her. Gasping, bent over, she rested for a moment. Listening to hear if he was following, but the night was still, except for the lapping of water against the bank not far from her feet. And the rasping of her breath as she tried to calm herself.

When her heartbeat slowed, and her breaths became deep and regulated, she continued.

Only now noticing how cool the night had become, she started shaking. And her head spun threatening to floor her. She squinted her eyes shut to rid the stars in her vision. Was she going the right way?

Seeing the Kendal's path, she scrambled on her hands and knees up the bank to the yard. She had made it. Getting to her feet, she stumbled to the service door, banging loudly enough to wake the household. She waited in silence for the occupants to answer.

With great relief, she was ushered inside as soon as her employer opened the door and spied her battered profile looking back at him.

The Kendals offered refuge and support to May and she stayed on and did not return home.

Cinderella's punishment for not obeying was the loss of a shoe and her mode of transport. May's punishment was the loss of a tooth and nearly her life.

***

MAY MEETS CYRIL AGAIN

May continued to board with and work for the Kendals. Harvey had not been charged with assault for his attack on her, even at the insistence of Margret Kendal. May preferred to just distance herself from his presence.

Feeling remorseful, her mother came to visit her over the coming weeks, pleading with May to forgive her.

After much duress, May finally forgave her mother. But she would not visit the farm unless she knew Harvey was absent. Besides, she told her mother there was too much work for her to do here at the moment while the painters spruced up the Kendal homestead. She had to pack many tea chests full of trinkets and domestic junk from the Kendal's shelves and cupboards in readiness for the tradesmen.

Life was never boring here at the homestead, as there was something different to do every day. She'd much rather work inside instead of being out in the garden on the farm.

Some weekends, Lilly and Virginia would hurry their chores and come over to visit her. They'd sit out on the lawn at the back of the property near the river. The same area she had come up from the river that night of the dance.

They told her Alina and Bonnie were constantly asking to see her. It made her sad to think that her sisters were missing her, but she could not go back to that violence. She just couldn't.

One of the painters seemed to take an interest in her. She spied him watching her and realised it was Cyril, who quite obviously and rather embarrassing for May tried to attract her attention.

She had tried to get rid of him at the dance and here he was still bothering her.

She had to be polite while at work, but she'd soon let him know she wasn't interested in any man at all. She'd had enough violent beatings from the other gender.

May tried to pay him no heed as she went about her work.

'Hey May, aren't you going to talk to this good-looking Pommy bloke?' he'd joke with her.

'You're very pretty. Just my type.'

May had never been told she was pretty before. She'd always felt so ugly.

Her blonde wavy shoulder length hair had not been styled since the dance. And her pale blue eyes she thought could have been darker. Pretty? She didn't think so. Clearly, he was just a flirt. There weren't many pretty features on her face.

She did however like her white porcelain skin. It was smooth and not pockmarked with acne like some of the teens she'd seen.

Her figure was curvaceous and well-developed for her sixteen years. It embarrassed her and she tried to hide it under her modest clothing. She didn't want any of his unwelcome advances.

His pretend airs and graces weren't impressing her at all.

One day, he asked her out.

'I don't go out with strange men,' she told him.

Cyril did not give up and set about making himself known to her mother down the road.

'He seems nice. A fine respectable English gentleman.' Antoinette pestered her during her next visit to the Kendal's. 'He's been out to the farm helping us out.'

May looked at her mother's broad smile, trying to read the intent. This was supposed to be just a friendly catch up, out in the back garden by the river.

She sat staring, glued to the wicker chair that had been placed on the grass along with its twin, earlier in the day, in readiness for her mother's visit.

'I don't like him. Besides he's much older than me,' she said to her mother.

'Don't be ridiculous. You know you won't find anyone else who will be so accepting of your past. You're lucky he still wants to see you. I've given him permission to see you,' Antoinette said.

'What!' Shame rattled through her. 'You told him everything?'

'Yes, I had to, didn't I? Best to be straight up at the start,' her mother said.

'How could you?' May frowned. 'Well I suppose it doesn't matter. You've told everyone else anyhow.'

'You will marry him, or you won't marry anyone. No-one will have you. This is a good opportunity and you should be grateful he is so accepting.'

May couldn't believe it. She was so angry with her mother and so embarrassed for herself. How could she face Cyril the painter ever again?

Oh, why did everything always turn to this. Always leading her back to her past. Her mind started clouding as those voices from within started sneering and taunting her.

Gotta get some work done,' said her mother, standing up to leave.

'Okay,' she blurted out after that degrading onslaught.

How could she?

***

CYRIL TELLS HIS STORY

Cyril arrived to pick her up. One of his mates had dropped him at the Kendal's, as he didn't drive.

He smiled and greeted her with a friendly peck on the cheek. 'Let's go for a walk over to see your mother. And you could show me around the farm. Haven't seen it all yet.'

She still didn't know why she had agreed to have him visit. Perhaps her mother was right. She *was* tarnished. Just a piece of rubbish.

She had run it through her mind and hadn't slept for nights. She was lucky he'd even taken any interest in her at all. Isn't that what Antoinette had told her? Well at least there'd be no secrets. He knew it all.

May had always dreamed of marriage and a family. Maybe she could still have a chance at the happy ever after. 'I'll get my things.'

She decided to take him out the back and along the river to the farm. The way she'd come on that dreadful night of the dance. In daytime it was pretty, and she fathomed he could deal with any snakes if they happened to see any.

It was a pleasant sunny day and May happily strolled along, enjoying the sounds of the wild birds in the gum trees as Cyril told her his story.

Resting on the branches of the old red gums that hung close to the ground, he started his tale.

***

THE LITTLE BOY FROM BIRMINGHAM

Cyril was the first-born son of Charlotte and Cyril Senior. He lived in Birmingham England, with four older sisters who ensured he always received plenty of female attention. His life started in a red brick, two storey house in Arlington Grove. An area for the Working-Class Poor. And his life was pretty typical for the times.

His parents worked in factories and caught a bus at the end of the street. Cyril had loved to play in the street with his sisters and from a young age, any stray child that entered Arlington

Grove uninvited was treated with contempt. And territorial fights would erupt. He enjoyed the fight. As did his mother. She was always on his side, rolling up her sleeves and knocking on the doors of the enemy. It was never his fault. That's what Cyril loved about her.

During the Second World War, the city of Birmingham became very dangerous. Afraid of aerial bombardment, the government ordered the mass evacuation of school-aged children. Operation Pied Piper as it was known, saw millions of children fostered out to unfamiliar places. And placed with total strangers.

Cyril could hear the sounds of the War. It was etched in his brain.

Cyril, along with five of his siblings, had to leave the city. His two younger brothers would stay with his parents in Birmingham. 'It is for your safety,' his father Cyril Senior explained. 'Some children have evacuated already. You will all adapt quickly and be safe until the war is finished. I will be waiting for you to return.'

Fear trundled through Cyril. He was always scared. He couldn't even sleep properly. He would be going with Brian and his four sisters. Goodness knows where? He was older than Brian, so he would have to look after his little brother. At least they had each other.

A well-meaning attempt from the British government to protect and continue educating its next generation, managed to fracture many households. On all sides, the feelings of separation and abandonment caused distress on leaving, and emotional anxiety and heartbreak on returning. Some children did not want to return home, having made a new life with loving foster families. A very difficult adjustment for all involved.

Brian didn't go with him and neither did his sisters. Cyril didn't know why. He hoped he would see his brother and his sisters again soon. After the War they would all meet together again. They could be pals again. And play ball in the street.

Would his street be there? Or his house? He was scared about the baby brothers he'd left at home and Mum and Dad. They were still being bombed. Would he ever see any of them again? Oh, the horror of it all. He couldn't forget the sounds. They haunted him in his sleep and occupied his thoughts in the daytime.

The assembly area was full of children just like his family. Cyril hadn't even realised there were so many students attending his school. Maybe it was the additional parents and teachers that crowded through the gates that added to the confusion he felt. He hung close to his family group, dreading what was to come.

He was wearing his new coat that his mum had bought him especially for his journey. He was pinned with a luggage label and issued his evacuation parcel. It contained his toiletries, a change of clothes, a pair of slippers, something to sleep in, and a gas mask in a small wooden box, just in case he came in contact with any toxic fumes.

Cyril hated his gas mask as much as anyone. The rubber was really annoying against his face. And it was hot and claustrophobic. But the worst thing was the smell of disinfectant that his mother cleaned the spittle with that accumulated inside it. Never mind that they were always fogging up and you couldn't see a thing.

Cyril was ushered out into the line-up with the rest of his family. Then sooner than anticipated, the family set off to the train station. And as he boarded the train, Mum and Dad waved him off on the platform and he headed out of Birmingham.

***

WALES

Children shifted around so much that the noise of chatter was distracting, so Cyril sat there silently for a while trying to block all the activity going on around him. And then when it became too much, the tears started. He was alone.

The reception area soon became crowded as they piled in off the train. And he was herded along with hundreds of other children and placed into groups. None of them really knew what was going on, as adults began pointing, looking, choosing.

Cyril sat on the floor, with his back up against the wall. Perhaps down here he could hide from this travesty.

He closed his eyes and plugged his ears with his pinkies. The popping sounds of the bombs, as the home defence tried desperately to knock the German planes from the skies, was a sound he could not forget. It threatened to drive him mad.

He could hear his father— 'Birmingham has become too dangerous. Not a place for children.' So he'd sent him here. In a room full of strangers. And he was very scared without any of his family.

He was taken to the Welsh Village of Ynysybwl (Un-is-u-bull). They were church people and compelled Cyril to attend a Methodist service every Sunday. He didn't really like going to church, but he wanted to please his foster parents, so he didn't complain. Cyril enjoyed the love of his foster family. Having no children of their own meant they devoted a lot time to him and were very understanding. Which helped him heal the scars of War. As he adjusted to village life in Wales, he grew to adore his foster mum Peggy, and she him.

Uncle Tomi worked long tedious hours in the coal mines, so Cyril spent most of his time with Peggy. Or playing in the street with the Welsh children like he had in Birmingham. Only this wasn't Birmingham. At times he really missed everyone. He wondered where they had all gone.

***

THE RAFT

Cyril had moved in with his new foster family. A two-up two-down stone terrace on New Road, in the village of Ynysybwl. After breakfast one clear morning, he was keen to finish his chores quickly. Some of the local lads were building a raft on the river and he wanted to see it launched.

'Aunt Peg, can I go outside to play?'

'Cyril, please go and make *ya gwely.'*

She meant *my bed.* I surprised myself that I had managed to learn a lot of the Welsh language in a short time.

'Ya should put ya dirty clothes in the washroom. Then you are free ta go. Mind ya in for lunch.'

He really loved Aunt Peg. She always doted on him and showed him kindness. He didn't like chores. But he wanted to please her by doing what he was told.

Excited at the prospect of spending time by the river, he raced up the stairs.

Eyeing his sleeping space, he saw the mess. His bedlinen dragging on the floor, and the eiderdown scrunched down at the foot of the bed. The pillow had moved and was wedged against the wall. He was still plagued by demons in the darkness of night. He shivered as his mind tried not to conjure up the images. This bed needed serious work. He had no time to reflect if he wanted to get to the river.

He wasn't very tall for six and his muscles weren't helping him. The blankets felt like a lead weight. Wales seemed colder than his beloved city of Birmingham. And the hills around the village made it darker somehow. He certainly needed thicker bed linen. Aunt Peggy always made sure he was as warm and comfortable as he could be. He did so want to please her. Struggling for what seemed like an eternity, he finally managed to finish the task.

Now gathering his new clothes that Peggy had made for him, Cyril tucked them under one arm. Turning, he surveyed the room. The bed resembled one of those Yorkshire puddings he'd seen Aunt Peggy make. Mm, not the best. But that would have to do. There were other priorities in a boy's life.

He yelled good-bye as he skidded out the back door and out into the field. Cyril arrived at the river well after the other boys. As he approached, he heard a buzz of activity. Not being familiar with any of the locals, he stood up on the bank to watch.

The other lads were in the process of damming the flow of water. This end of the river was a little shallower than the rest. But it was still fast flowing and deep in the middle. Leafy shrubs and trees lined the edges. The mosses still wet enough to cling to any shaded areas. The sun shone its beams on the rippling water.

Cyril stood looking. He couldn't believe his eyes. A very impressive whirlpool swirled in the middle of the river.

'We're ready to launch the raft!' yelled one of the other boys.

Gee he's tall. And he must be at least eleven. Or even twelve? The locals and quite a number of their friends had gathered to watch this momentous event.

'Who will volunteer?' someone shouted. 'We need someone to test the raft. Who is brave enough?'

Cyril wondered who would step forward and participate. He waited along with the others to witness this brave individual.

But after a few minutes, when no one was going to volunteer to do such a dangerous activity, one of the bigger boys shouted, 'How about that kid?'

Cyril spun round to see who was standing behind him. And who they were pointing at.

Within seconds, they'd surrounded him. Someone grabbed his collar. 'You can do it!'

'You little pommy bastard.'

'Now get on!'

They sneered, with their fists shoved in his face, and the look of derision on their faces, forcing Cyril to comply. Though scared and intimidated, what choice did he have? These boys were huge, and certainly outnumbered him. He would surely be beaten up if he refused.

They placed the raft on the river. Constructed of recycled oil drums, tied beneath a platform of old timber of varying stages of rotting, it looked rough at best. Cyril cringed, fear tightening his gut. His church prayers came in handy as he prayed like mad that he'd survive.

As they dragged him onto the vessel, the smell of damp rotting vegetation permeated his nostrils.

Bits of stick and small splintered logs floated and bobbed around, his senses on high alert.

What if he drowned here? Here in this little coal valley in South Wales. Would Aunt Peggy find him face down in the River? His lungs filled with iced mountain water. Maybe the bombs would have been a better death?

Trying to be as brave as the soldiers sent to war, he inhaled and climbed aboard. Grabbing on tightly to the frayed rope that had been attached to the battered raft, he closed his eyes as they gave the vessel an almighty shove. Cyril was off on the ride of a lifetime.

It terrified him. The sides of the platform began to sink. Cyril found it extremely difficult to hold on. His fear rose as the raft was immediately drawn towards the spiralling whirlpool. The thought of being sucked into the vortex made his head hurt.

If the raft flipped upside down, he would surely drown. The water flooded the boards he sat on and soaked his pants. Panic rose inside him as he neared the whirlpool. Was it time to abandon this ship? He tried to calm himself by focusing on the crowd that watched his voyage.

Were the Welsh boys starting to retreat? *I suppose they don't want to stay and get in strife for drowning the Pommy kid.*

'Oh no! I'm really going to die!' he screamed.

The raft popped up above the surface. Cyril managed to steer it away from the rapids, arriving safely back into the shallows.

A loud cheer rang out and everyone was ecstatic. The raft was river-worthy.

And Cyril was the hero of the day.

***

A MOVE TO AUSTRALIA

At the end of the war there were parties in the streets, and Arlington Grove had their own. But not everyone adapted easily.

When Cyril arrived home, it was very upsetting to his younger brother George, who had been a toddler when Cyril had left the city all those years ago. 'Who are ya?' George sneered at Cyril.

'Tis all right pet, 'tis our Cyril,' Charlotte told him.

'No, he ain't. Clear off before I snot ya,' he said to Cyril.

Cyril tried to explain his years of absence to George. But George was angry and plotted to gather his mates together and scrap with Cyril. But Cyril was tipped off and belted his brother instead. Not a nice welcome home for all.

Cyril's years in the Wales countryside had been a life of freedom roaming with the Welsh village boys. It was here he learnt to fight and fend for himself. He'd even been involved in nearly burning down the village. He never told anyone that he was there, or else Peggy and Tomi would be mad with him.

His friends hadn't meant for the fire to spread so rapidly through the grass. But that is what happened. Cyril hadn't lit the fire, but he knew who had, and he wasn't going to tell.

Cyril had missed playing ball in the street with Brian and had longed to resume their relationship on his return home. And for a short while they did get to kick the footy. But sadly, things between them were not the same as before the war. They had grown apart during their years away and Cyril knew he had become harder somehow.

The war had changed him and Brian as well. Even the streets looked different from how he'd remembered them. Both he and his brother were no longer interested in the same things. Brian, unlike himself, had not been happy in his billeted house.

Brian never wanted to talk about it and Cyril never prompted him.

Cyril's sisters were past childhood games and had started working in the factories.

Brian was distant and getting into trouble, Cyril's younger brothers didn't really know him, and his parents were like strangers.

He resumed his schooling for a while, but it was hard as his life was so different here in Birmingham. He felt restless like he no longer belonged.

As soon as he was old enough to join the national service, he gave it a try. Cyril loved the thought of serving his country, but he really didn't like the discipline and the strict training it entailed, and decided it wasn't for him.

He felt like a lost soul. The war had disrupted his life and now he was having trouble working out where he belonged.

He decided to sail to Australia. The brochures promised him plenty of work for good money, and a couple of his mates were going. He figured he had nothing to lose.

So, Cyril said goodbye again to his family and boarded a ship to Australia.

In his new country he would be known as a Ten Pound Pom.

***

MAY AND CYRIL

Cyril's story flabbergasted May. They had been sitting together on the limbs of the red gums engrossed in conversation. Cyril was quite a storyteller. At least 40 minutes had passed, and they continued on their way to the farm. May showed him the way as he insisted on holding her hand.

Arriving at the well-worn track that led to the house, she negotiated the steep incline. Cyril clung on close behind. Reaching the top, she gingerly looked around. *She didn't want her first visit back to her home since the dance, to be a confrontation with Harvey. She had come to see her mother and her little sisters.* Frank would be working so she'd catch up with him at a later date.

Alina was the first to appear. Running up and wrapping her arms around her sister. 'May,' she cried out. 'May! How I've missed you!' Her eyes welled up with tears.

May loved Alina, a quiet, emotional child, with a kind heart. Years of violence had made her timid and shy. 'Come, and we will find Virginia and Lilly.'

Is he your boyfriend?' Alina said, pointing her finger at Cyril.

'Just a friend,' May said, also to not give him any doubt about her intentions.

May spotted Virginia and Lilly down near the chicken coops filling the grain bins. They came running up to her in excitement. Both talking at once and dancing around her. Chattering at top speed.

'Slow down, I want you to say hi to Cyril. And no, he's not my boyfriend!' S*he'd better stop saying that, he'd think she was rude.* And she hated when people were rude to her.

'I soon will be though,' Cyril said with confidence.

He may have made up his mind, but she still wasn't sure. She couldn't shake off the underlying dread. It was all happening so fast.

'Come on, Mum has Bonnie inside,' Lilly said.

'Where's Harvey?'

'Don't worry he's in town today. Mother sent him in to do some errands.' Virginia smiled.

That eased May a little. 'Okay but let's show Cyril the farm first. He's awful keen,' she said.

Cyril behaved like a gentleman and walked happily beside her, as her sisters showed him every corner of the property.

Antoinette called them from the house with an invitation for lunch. And Cyril said how impressed he was as everyone enjoyed plates of boiled eggs with cucumber, tomato and beetroot salad. All fresh produce they grew and prepared on the farm.

May relished the merriment of the moment and her heart filled with warmth for her loved ones.

Antoinette's conversation with Cyril enabled May to pay attention to the little one. Bonnie sat on her knee for cuddles.

And then, May had had enough, and it was time to go. *It must be time for Harvey to return. He might kill me this time. Get out quick before he comes.* Her mind raced, and her anxiety quickly escalated.

How long had she been here? She didn't want to run into him. The memory of that terrible night of the dance suddenly flooded back to her.

It was a pleasant couple of hours spent with her beloved sisters. The separation had been hard for all of them.

Placing Bonnie on the floor, she stood up. 'We really must get going now.'

'Can't you stay longer. Please, May.' Bonnie looked sad and her bottom lip quivered. She tried to get back up on May's knee for more affection.

'I would if I could, Bon. But I've got to get Cyril back to catch his ride home.'

'It's not fair!' Bonnie stamped her foot and bit her bottom lip.

But May could not be swayed and bade them goodbye. Promising Bonnie she'd return soon, she headed up the driveway and out the front gate with Cyril.

***

NOT SUCH A GENTLEMAN

May agreed to see Cyril and in the coming months, he became a familiar visitor. But the shine soon wore off for her when he attempted to force her into intimate relations. Cyril started to pressure— even bully— her into giving in. It extremely upset May and she told Antoinette that she wanted to end their relationship.

'Don't be foolish. Who else will want you?' were Antoinette's hurtful words to her whenever she approached the subject. 'He wants to marry you. You won't find anyone else. I insist that you do.'

For weeks May didn't give up. 'But he's nasty to me. He has a bad temper. I don't want to marry him!'

But it mattered not to either. Between the two they had made up their minds. They just wouldn't listen.

Her sisters had begun to witness Cyril's temper and he'd threatened them, told them to stay away whenever he was visiting. 'I want to be alone with May,' he'd tell them. 'So leave us alone.'

Cyril had managed to persuade her mother that he was the right suitor and Antoinette's insistence and constant bickering wore away at her. Eventually, she just gave in. May, again feeling powerless and bullied, agreed to their arrangement. Her whole life had been about dominance and this wasn't any different.

Her father had beaten her so badly one time that her legs had been covered in blood. Whip marks from the stick he had struck her with had broken the skin on her thighs and calves. She could close her eyes and still conjure up that frightening memory.

Afraid of being exposed, her parents had kept her home from school on the pretence that she had been nursing a fever from a childhood disease. Giving them time to heal.

But in reality, the scars had never healed. They were still there, along with all the rest of them. Just under the surface, she could feel them rubbing like scarred tissue in her mind. Her young life had broken her. May knew she was damaged. She might never find love.

***

MARRIAGE

May decided to move to the south of Deniliquin, and secured employment in the Steam Laundry. This enabled her to rent a small flat in the town and save a little money towards her wedding. As Cyril didn't drive, this decision meant that at least she could see more of him and try to get to know him a little better.

As the days drew nearer, pre-wedding nerves created uncertainty for May, and she begged Antoinette to cancel. But her mother was adamant that the wedding would proceed.

Cyril and May got married in spring. On the day of her wedding, May's twin bridesmaids tried to calm her, but to no avail.

May borrowed her lovely cream satin gown from a work friend. It fitted her perfectly and she was blown away when she saw her reflection. With a fitted bodice and full-length sleeves, its long satin train flowed like rippled water as she walked. For the first time in her life, she felt beautiful. Every girl dreamed of the fairy-tale wedding and May had often fantasised the dream.

But she couldn't shake off the impending doom. It was true that Cyril had been a little better of late, but he was at the pub till closing some nights after work. It was a man's right after all. He'd recited it to her on many a day. No women allowed at the pub, of course.

In a silent act of defiance, May got drunk and swaggered down the aisle of the church. Reciting her vows with slurred speech and a numbed soul, she married Cyril the Englishman, who dressed in a black dinner suit with a white carnation in his lapel and matching white gloves.

But looks can be deceiving. And she just wanted it to be over.

***

BIRTH AND DEATH

May married Cyril, and in the months that followed, her mother Antoinette delivered a new baby sister, Martha. No one really thought she looked like any of them. May said she took her father's looks. And Harvey said that was just fine.

There was plenty of help from Lilly and Virginia who really enjoyed a new baby to cuddle and care for. They just added Martha to their already busy schedule and proceeded as normal.

May and Cyril were eventually blessed with three little girls. There was one more baby girl, however. A little newborn with its pink smooth skin covered in Vernix, the white waxy substance that tends to accumulate in the folds of its body just after birth, before hospital staff time to bathe it. Pink! Or was her skin blue. With lips to match. May didn't know. And she didn't want to talk about the details.

Caroline was May and Cyril's first born. But their firstborn had died soon after birth. *Haemorrhaging* was the word the medical staff used. How could that be? How was her baby born alive and then haemorrhage and die? May didn't understand.

Maybe it was a rare Vitamin K deficiency.

Or maybe her newborn had suffered a stroke, or the nurses damaged her with birthing tools. She hadn't seen them drop her.

Whatever the cause, May never actually found out the truth. It was too painful to go over, and no-one wanted to talk about it.

It was a terrible time. Their time of dreams had turned into a nightmare. Their daughter's death was the beginning of the unravelling of a doomed marriage. Adding layers to their heartache.

May's world fell apart. Her distress at losing Caroline saw her spending many hours by the graveside, crying. Her grief compounded by the fact that she had been denied the chance to look into her child's tiny face. They had not allowed her any cradling. No soft kisses. No touching. Not even a peep. And most certainly, no joy.

The cemetery was a long way from town to trudge, but it was here that she felt connected to her child. Here she could talk to Caroline just like she used to talk to her sisters buried in the valley.

Her baby's isolated dirt mound held no headstone. Just a metal black marker with her number stamped. Without her name engraved, who would even know she existed.

May, like her mother, had buried her angel. Caroline would live in Heaven now with May's twin sisters. And one day they would all be there to meet her.

For weeks, her loss consumed her every waking hour and she begged her mother to allow her to bring Martha home to stay a while. She was sure looking after her baby sister would help keep her busy and take her mind off her pain.

Antoinette agreed and she had brought Martha home. But Cyril had been angry at May and had shown no understanding. He had yelled at her and forced her to take Martha back to the farm. And depression consumed May again.

***

MAY'S THREE GIRLS

May had three more little girls after her heavenly angel, all of them born close in age.

Robyn, her first, had a shot of dark hair with the sweetest little features. May loved her instantly. But Robyn was a fussy eater and at times she found her difficult to handle.

She tried to get her husband to help with the baby a little more. 'Being a new mother is exhausting,' she'd tell him. But it was like he wasn't paying attention or just chose to ignore her plight. She still had days of depression, with the loss of Caroline still raw like an open wound.

Frequently, she walked Robyn out to the gravesite in the pram to visit the mound. May was scared she'd forget Caroline and she didn't want to.

And she found herself pregnant again with a new baby on the way.

Her second daughter, Linda was born in the summer only thirteen months after Robyn. While she was resting from her labour, Cyril was escorted to see his prize. He said he didn't mind that they had another little girl. But after trudging up to the nursery to see her, he wasn't pleased at all. Storming into the ward, he started ranting. 'She's not mine. She has red hair. Who's the father?' He sneered at her, insinuating she'd committed adultery.

'She's yours of course!' May said firmly, trying hard to hold back tears of hurt and anger. She was gutted.

Why was her husband being so cruel and thoughtless? They started to argue as she tried to defend her honour. 'Get out!' She screeched. 'Until you've thought about your actions.'

May's world crumbled. Instead of celebrating the joy of their new baby girl, there was suspicion and argument.

Cyril did return to the hospital, perhaps to try to amend his stupidity towards her. But there was never an apology and May would never forget his bitter words.

She took the baby home, and everyone said how much Linda looked like her father. Which you could plainly see. And of course, he grew to love her too.

With two little ones to care for now, May was kept busy and visited the gravesite less.

Domestic chores and parenting duties took up her time. But still occasionally, she would enjoy a walk to the cemetery, where she would add flowers and ponder her life. Laying baby Linda in the pram with Robyn on the little carry seat, she'd set off through the harsh flat landscape, enjoying its solitude.

'I'm pregnant again!' she told her husband.

'What! How did you manage that? You're always pregnant.' He rolled his eyes.

His words were hurtful, ignorant. She lifted her chin. 'How do you think?'

'Bloody hell woman, you're useless.' He sneered at her.

It was on, but that was nothing new. They often fought. Especially if he'd been drinking down at the pub and arrived home drunk. He never took any responsibility or even part of the blame for anything.

She was frustrated, sick of it, but powerless to change it. With another baby on the way, she was compelled to just continue on as best she could.

Regardless of his attitude at having a new baby, Rhonda was born six months later.

May allowed him to name their baby. He named her Rhonda, after the Rhondda River that flowed through the village of Ynysybwl during his childhood in Wales.

May's depression and hopelessness at having to cope with another newborn nearly became too much. A sweet little baby with the finest cover of blonde hair, practically bald, Rhonda suffered from reflux. She challenged May's sanity even more, with days of restlessness and nights of dread as Rhonda would scream and vomit up bottles of milk for a good part of her day.

May was near breaking point caring for three babies under the age of three with a husband not interested in sharing the domestic duties.

***

AN AXE FOR DINNER

Cyril was not the best husband to May.

She resented him for not helping her when she needed him. And he never supplied her and the children with enough housekeeping money to meet their needs. He kept a tight budget. Except of course when it came to buying his beer or gambling on the horses.

Cyril liked to drink ale. A Pommy trait he'd brought with him to Australia. With Deniliquin's hot climate, it was easy to understand the need to cool off after work. But much to May's annoyance, Cyril regularly engaged in an after-work session at the pub, downing as many as he could in the short time available and arriving home bloody good-for-nothing. It infuriated her, and she was sure he delighted in her misery.

She and the children seemed to be always waiting for him to arrive home. Robyn especially whined for her father. His favouritism of her ensured her loyalty. And May got no peace until he was safely home.

"It's my right to enjoy a drink at the pub if I feel like it," was his constant one-liner that he'd recite to her. His ignorance to entitlement guaranteed her resentment.

May was tired. Being so close in age, her three little girls took a lot of looking after. It really was arduous and dealing with Cyril's drunkenness always upset everyone. May often reflected on her current situation and admitted to herself that it had been a mistake to marry him. He certainly had a bad temper when he wanted.

May needed wood to cook their dinner. There were still some logs down by the old laundry, but they were impossible for May to split. She had tried, but the axe wouldn't cut through the knots grown in the grain of the wood. She had waited days for Cyril to sort out the problem and couldn't wait any longer.

She didn't have wood to light the heater for the tank over the bath either and had washed the girls in the wading pool this afternoon. The water out the back had warmed enough in the sun to make it bearable, but this was getting ridiculous.

May hadn't been able to light the stove since using up the scrap bark she'd raked off the ground down by the stack this morning. And yesterday they'd gone for a walk to the river, and the girls had helped her gather up sticks and a couple of small limbs that had fallen to the ground from ants.

She'd brushed off the crawlers and wrapped the wood in an old baby blanket. Pushing the bundle home in the pram with Rhonda. Even so, the stove hadn't stayed alight for too long before it burnt down to cinders.

The girls and her had eaten cold leftovers and bottled stewed fruit from her mother's farm stores tonight. And May decided she'd teach that ignorant bastard Cyril a lesson. She wouldn't cook him anything tonight. *See how he liked them eggs.*

Feeling defiant and frustrated, May decided to serve him the axe for dinner. Giggling to herself and feeling smug about her plan, she lay its head on a large plate, with its handle hanging over the edge. The axe took up nearly the width of the small table.

That will do it. She waited.

A short time later, while May was getting the children into bed, the back door opened, and Cyril stumbled in.

'What's for tea, luv?' he said in his English accent.

'It's dished out on the table.' She pointed to the axe, not paying him too much attention.

'What the hell's this?' he mumbled under his under his breath as he spied the axe. His disapproval obvious.

'It's your dinner, of course. You haven't chopped the wood for me to light the fire. So, you don't have any dinner until I can cook again. And there's the axe. Now go use it on them stumps out there.'

May knew she might cop one, but how else could she get her point across. He never really took her seriously. Now maybe he would.

'You smart bitch!' He cursed, knocking the chair over as he tried to grab her.

But May was fast as lightning. Realising he wasn't in the mood for jokes, she raced to her bedroom and slammed the door. *After all, things could easily get out of hand with the axe sitting on the table.*

May moved fast, making a barrier by barring the door with a small cupboard pushed against it. Not a moment too soon. He thumped at the door while she cowered on the bed.

Robyn had wandered out to see what all the noise was about and distracted Cyril from his rant. He ordered her to bed while he rummaged through the cupboards looking for food, finally settling on whatever he could find. A short time later, he was passed out on the couch. And all was peaceful except for the odd snort as he positioned his body in his fitful sleep.

There were many incidents of drunken arguments, fighting and violence, days of depression and hopelessness for May. And her three little girls were there amongst the madness and the crying and the nights when she was locked outside in the dark. The nights when he would scream at them if they dared tell him to leave their mummy alone.

She had to hang on for now, wondering where they would go, and how they would survive. So, she stayed a while longer. Going back to the laundry for a few hours a week enabled her to save some money to buy a car. May's sisters helped with her daughters. And she set about learning how to drive.

There were some happy moments however, and excitement came in the form of a bank loan.

May and Cyril purchased two blocks of land. Having two blocks side by side would give them extra room to grow a few vegetables and perhaps her mother could breed her up some chickens for the girls to look after. The promise of a new home and more room excited May. She had never owned anything in her entire life. *Perhaps,* she dared to dream, *things would work out and life would settle.*

But it was not to be, and one drunken night, he threw all the house documents into the stove fire. May watched in dismay, unable to rescue them from the embers.

Her husband vowed they'd never build a house.

May was crushed. Her dreams dashed, burnt in the cinders like a sinner to the devil. It was evil, pure evil, to treat her that way, and she would never forget his sin.

From that day on she cast aside her marriage and future with Cyril, waiting her chance to flee.

***

VISITING THE FARM

I am nearing four years old and my life is woven into my Grandmother's farm. It is here where I make special bonds with my child aunts. I'm learning about our family's struggles and the invisible threads that connect us all. I am Linda.

'Today we'll go to the farm, and I can practise my driving,' said Mother.

My sister, Robyn loved to scale Grandma's fruit trees. She was agile, so climbing came easy. Getting down however was another matter, and she was constantly squawking to get down. I was sure she just loved attention.

I was not a climber, preferring instead to have my feet firmly on the earth. Watching from the ground seemed a lot safer to me. Seeing my sister stuck on a branch screaming her lungs out, certainly influenced my reluctance.

We'd woken early as usual, so Mother drove us out to the farm after breakfast. Her driving skills still needed some refinement. She often missed a gear, which put us at risk of falling off the seats with all the jerking and stopping and starting as she kangaroo-hopped along the road. But that didn't matter, we still enjoyed our new mode of transport. And it certainly beat walking.

Mother pulled off the road onto the gravel. 'Robyn, get out and open the gate please,' she said.

'Oh, why do I have to do it?' Robyn said, as she screwed up her pretty little pixie face and sneered at me.

I didn't care. I knew I wasn't expected to oblige.

'Linda's too small to work out the chain. You're a big girl,' Mother told her. 'You know how to line the ring up.'

'It's not fair, I always do it.'

'You're such a good helper.' Mother kept up the praise, knowing that tactic always worked. 'Come on, get out, and help Mum.'

Her words did the trick as Robyn bounced her tiny frame off the bench-seat and out the door.

With a little persistence, she managed to unlock and swing the gate wide. And a few seconds later, Mother pressed the accelerator and we moved forward into the dusty driveway of my Grandmother's property.

After latching the chain back into place, Robyn climbed back in. Sticking out her tongue, she then scolded me. 'When you get bigger, you will have to do it! And I will sit on my bum just like you.'

I just poked my tongue back at her, not even giving it another thought.

My eldest sister was a beauty. With tiny little features— small green eyes, a cute little turned up nose and high cheek bones. Her hair smooth and shiny, the colour of straw. Straight enough to look immaculate, but with plenty of bounce so it sat softly around her face. Her olive complexion flawless. Her body petite with skinny little limbs.

I loved her but she didn't always treat me well. Maybe thirteen months isn't enough time alone with your parents when you are the first-born. Robyn was a Daddy's girl and my father's favourite. Her bond with our mother was not the same as the bond with our father.

My auburn curly hair and green eyes guaranteed I got more than my share of attention. By the age of four, my locks were so long and thick that I often complained of headaches, so Mum had it cut. I couldn't go anywhere without complete strangers cooing and complimenting me on my looks. I'm sure that didn't make my sister like me any better.

Taller and with a more athletic build than me, Robyn teased me for being the chubby one. Using hurtful words to intimidate me, she called me "Fats" as we got older. Her relentless taunting chipped away at my self-esteem. Yes, I was fatter than her, but only because Robyn was so very thin.

Eventually I got my revenge by calling her bandy legs. Robyn didn't take too kindly to being teased herself, and I would cop a violent hair-pulling event every time. But I figured it was worth it to get some of my own back.

My grandmother had a new house, built from cement sheeting to make sure it stood up to white ant infestation. It was much bigger, and better equipped than the previous cottage, which no longer existed. The rooms had been eaten by ants and had become dangerous. Whatever was left had been burnt to ensure the extermination of the destructive pest.

The car moved forward down the driveway and passed the vegetable garden and orchard on the left. They rounded the bend in the gravel. Lined up side by side and backing onto the river, the home-made cages where all the feathered animals were housed came into sight.

Grandma owned turkeys. Strange creatures with their flaps of loose neck skin wobbling around like jelly. They'd strut around with their tails fanned out, just daring anyone to challenge them, and making their weird alien sounds. "Gobble gobble gobble gobble." We children would laugh at their ridiculous antics and mimic their calls.

On this cool crisp morning, my sisters and I wound down the window and shouted, "Gobble gobble gobble." All three of us. My baby sister too.

Rhonda was just starting to understand our little game. We all rolled around laughing on the back seat in good humour. Mother laughed too; she always saw the funny side.

The car came to a halt only seconds before my aunts came running out of the house.

Bonnie was first. She was one of my favourites. With thin mousy hair and a tiny face to match her small frame. Petite was what she was. But she could tumble her words out at record speed. Her order in the family meant if she hesitated, her conversation would be lost in the babble of her older sisters.

'Come on, Rob! Come and help me with the chooks. I've got to feed them and then check for any eggs.' Bonnie flung open the door of the vehicle and Robyn jumped out.

Alina had heard us talking and arrived to help. A quiet, timid young lady, she had learnt to stay out of the way of conflict. Very fragile in nature, she lacked confidence and was easily upset.

She found solace and companionship at the Salvation Army, attending the Sunday school. Bonnie went too, and sometimes they would take Martha, Robyn and me. We loved to colour in or paste pictures of Jesus or one of the disciples. Everyone would sing hymns and clap to the tunes. The brass band played the notes and the tambourines set the rhythm.

'I'll bring Lindy Lou,' said Alina using my pet name. She called after Bonnie, as I made my way out of the vehicle.

Robyn and Bonnie had run off down the dusty track towards the chicken coop.

The poultry cages were a work of art, nailed together with scrounged timber, with buckled chicken wire stretched and nailed across their framework. Galvanised sheets of tin, strategically placed in the back ends of the pens, provided shelter from the wind. Little nesting boxes dotted around the inside and nails held them in place.

It was quite snug and had been built sturdy to give each bird the protection needed from foxes, dogs or poisonous snakes.

Chickens, turkeys and ducks lived in the condos next door. Each pen had its own dirt-covered floor and tin bedroom suite covered in a rust pattern finish. Their outlook faced the driveway to capture a view through the mesh of incoming visitors.

'Come on, let's check for eggs,' Alina said. She strolled with me to the chook house, while Mother unloaded her jumble of things.

Rhonda climbed the steps, going up on all fours. She would stay in the house with Mother. With the river barely metres from the house, she was too young to wander without supervision. "People have drowned in that river," Grandma would constantly harp on at everyone.

My youngest sister Rhonda had snowy blond hair as fine as floating cobwebs. She had been born practically bald, and still only had a fine coating. Just enough hair so anyone who kissed her head to want to sweep their lips gently through it.

Her cute round face reflected pink, from the colour of her cheeks. Her green eyes matching all the sisters', a genetic trait inherited from our father. Everyone loved Rhonda as she was easy going and never any trouble.

Mother had thrown in a spare pair of trousers into her basket. She'd sewn them for us on her machine. She also added a knitted jumper that Granny had made. It hadn't mattered what size Grandma knitted, as long as the sleeves were the length of Robyn's arms, and the body wider for me, we could share. My sister had extra room to move while the sleeves just needed rolling up a little for me.

Mother had remembered to return the preserving jars from our last visit, unloading them from the car, along with a cake she had baked for Grandma's birthday.

On that cool August morning, the chickens weren't keen to leave their sheltered enclosure as we entered and left the door open. It wasn't the cleanest coup today. The stench was not at all pleasant. The rain had soaked the ground through the wire yesterday, and the chickens had churned it up into a slurry of bird faeces.

In the neighbouring pen, the ducks were even worse. Mud for them seemed a true heavenly delight. They had managed to make real mud pies, their features caked in dirt and their white feathers splattered in grime. Each one looked like they had just emerged from Rotorua's famous Polynesian spa. With so much mud plastered on their webbed feet, it was amazing they could even walk.

We walked back away from the pen and began tossing the scraps onto the ground outside. We would have to fill the pallet bins, but for now we just needed to entice the chickens out.

Seeing the vegetable peelings and leftover scraps were suddenly enough to have them race each other at lightning speed. Their heads pushed forward and their rear ends swayed side to side in a bid to outrun their competitors. An entertaining frenzy of pecking and tossing and wing flapping followed.

"Funny Chickens." Robyn chuckled.

Martha arrived to join us. Being only a few years older than us, meant we all played together. After we all helped fill the bins with pallets, Bonnie, Robyn and Alina carried the chook eggs back to the house.

Grandma was making tea in the kitchen and had dressed the metal teapot with an old crocheted woollen cosy she had made years before. She needed a new one, but it really wasn't on her list of priorities. As her guests waited for the tea, she skimmed the cream off the milk.

Before long, we got the shout for lunch, and sprinted inside to wash. Grandma never let us eat anything without washing our hands first. "You'll get worms if you don't," she'd always say to us. I didn't want worms, that's for sure, so I obeyed her instructions.

I learnt most of my old sayings and superstitions from Antoinette. I swear I was scared of her during my childhood. She was loud, swore like a trouper and had no filter when it came to expressing her point of view.

Grandma had no trouble slaughtering meat for her family. I found this barbaric and it really upset me. But Grandma didn't care if you witnessed the act. In fact, she kinda got off on it if you showed revulsion. I quickly learnt not to follow her around.

She'd have my aunts plucking feathers off dead poultry in the sink, the bath and the laundry. Down feathers floating in the air as my aunts worked alongside her. They hated it as much as I. But they had no way of escaping the task.

Not wanting to see more than I needed, I would not venture near the sinks. And would instead sit and play cards on the lounge floor. It was hard to block it out when it was going on all around you.

Not today, however. Today the house smelt like fruit salad. Preparing fruit to bottle was hard work, especially peeling, slicing and cutting out any bug holes. The bottles were like works of art. Filled to the brim with fruit, sugar and water. Their contents secured with a rubber ring and a metal clamp, and then placed in a boiler pot on the stove.

I knew what to do as I had participated before, even though I was only four then.

The fruit jars were already cooking when I walked in. All the hard work done. I only hoped we'd be taking some of that delicious produce home when we left.

We took off to the bedrooms with our aunts for playtime, while the adults finished off in the kitchen. It was still very cold outside, and we'd have to be content with inside activities. Martha had dried knuckle bones on the kitchen windowsill. Collecting them for weeks to gather enough for a game of knuckles.

Of course Aunt Martha won, as her hands were the biggest, which made picking them up and catching them much easier.

I didn't mind, but Robyn did. She hated losing.

Returning to the kitchen room sometime later, I found it filled with chatter and noise. We ate a hearty meal of homemade soup, damper bread, and stewed pears with cow cream. And then it was finally time for the Birthday song.

***

LEAVING FAMILY

May called Taxi Bernie. Any kid in town who rode a taxi, knew Bernie. He was the nice guy that carried a tin of treacle in his car. He'd dip his spoon in the delicious black syrup, swirl it skilfully, and quickly pop it into your mouth. "Yummy," we'd tell him.

Little did we know that spoon not only went into our mouths but every other child passenger he'd transported that year.

May was ending the marriage with Cyril, but it wasn't because of Taxi Bernie. Pity! We could have eaten treacle on every day of the week.

It was over and she was leaving Deniliquin with her newfound friend.

She had known him for a while now, as he lived in the house directly behind her. Her beloved Labrador had been constantly escaping through the holes in the broken palings, ensuring her a flirting contact.

They often stood and chatted over the low wooden stakes and tacked together bits of timber that vaguely resembled a fence.

Cyril was to blame. All could have been avoided by a little home maintenance.

Bruce was kind and offered her comfort and hope, especially since the loss of Sandy the Lab. He had heard the fighting too, she was sure. Only he was too polite to mention the accounts, or any of the details, his disgust hard to hide though when she had informed him of her regular lockouts.

His interest and attentiveness only compounded her thoughts of escape. It was only a matter of time.

The black doom was threatening to envelop her again as her depression built. Only a few months ago, she had taken a handful of pills, wanting to end it all for good. But then in her drug-induced state, she had remembered her beautiful little daughters. Creating harm for them, if she didn't make it. Would she be just like her father? Destroying their lives, like he had hers. She couldn't bear to think of such a thing.

It was through the haze that she had clawed her way back from the devil's grasp, just in time. If she had closed off her mind and drifted to sleep beside the sunbeams in her dreams, she would not be here. It was not Nirvana, she now knew. Just disguise and deception. All fire and hell. And she had nearly fallen for it.

But she had recovered. Together their love was mutual, and May wanted more than anything, to believe she deserved happiness. Bruce had promised her better and she was going to take a chance.

'You can live here.' Antoinette had offered her genuine support for once. (Maybe her guilt for pressuring May to marry.) There had been other horrific things she had subjected her daughter to as well. The worst by far was the recent killing of her Labrador. To May that was the final straw.

Offers of help to build a house by the river, were of no interest to May. She would never return to a life of slavery and violence. How could her mother even think she would live here?

May would make her own decisions this time.

She had argued with her mother and both said words they'd regret.

Bruce was her knight in shining armour, come to rescue her from the darkness and the doom. Her new love. Her friend.

Bruce held a lot of promise, and she hoped he wouldn't let her down.

She said goodbye to her beloved sisters but promised to return to see them when all this mess was sorted.

***

PART TWO:
A COLOURFUL LIFE

NIGHTMARES

His surname was Bruce. May called us Bruce. I wasn't sure if this decision was instant or whether the thought came to her later on. Maybe Mother thought the name would bond us all together. But I think, more likely, she wanted anonymity.

I had already learnt how to write my first name, but I hadn't even considered my surname.

May had experienced a lifetime of violence. I think Bruce gave her the courage to escape her old life and start anew. Even with all the abuse she had suffered at the hands of men, she still showed faith and perhaps believed in the happy ever after.

During the time of her breakdown, when she had wanted to end it all, my sisters and I had been taken to Grandma's farm.

As May got her treatment, I fretted and mourned for her presence.

My young life in disarray, I didn't understand what was really going on. But I heard them talk about May. Did they not care that I could hear their gossip and their judgment as I resided there?

It was not a secret. Nothing ever was in my family. Their verbal diarrhoea spilled from their foul mouths, spreading the rumours like a virus. And the murder of our pet a true reflection of the evil I believed existed in the depths of my Grandmother's soul.

If not for my aunts and the love of my sisters *(who were struggling too)* I would have had a total breakdown myself. As a child, I didn't know how to express my grief. I had no voice and no options open to me.

There had been arguments for weeks before my mother had become sick.

On a bad night he'd push her out and locked the door. She'd curled up in our cubby or sleep amongst the dirty washing on the old laundry floor.

One night he locked me out as well. I had bravely told him to leave my mummy alone. "You shut up," he'd snapped back at me.'

There we were, together in the dark.

We had pounded on the door and yelled at him to let us in, but he was drunk and yelled out to us that he didn't give a shit.

May put clothes over my pyjamas. My checked tent dress from yesterday— the one with the bow collar. I could still smell the strawberry jelly I'd spilt down the front and it was making me feel hungry.

Next, a grungy pair of tights with a ladder up the side, put there when I'd tried to pull them up the other day. And finally, a woollen jumper belonging to Robyn, its sleeves so long I couldn't find my hands.

Mother had stored a few old cushions in the corner after her first lockout, never wanting to be caught short again if she happened to find herself in a similar situation.

Placing them on top of the washing pile, we settled in for a fitful sleep.

And now here I was out on the farm without my mother. My distress was sending me mad with nightmares.

The fat man of my dreams would chase me. Running frantically, I was so terrified he would catch me. I could hear him behind me as I turned my head to look. He snarled and bared his teeth at me in anger.

Because of his massive bulk, he was puffed, and I could hear his laboured breathing. *(Probably too fat to run.)*

He was enjoying the chase and started to taunt me. Faaat.

With a menacing voice and eyes of pure evil, he terrified me.

Suddenly he shrank and became very thin in front of my eyes, his voice a horror whisper. Skinneee.

I stopped to watch the change, but the thin man started to chase me, too.

I was back to racing at full speed, until I couldn't run anymore. Then he changed back to the fat man. Faaat.

Then thin again. Skinneee.

The nightmare continued, with the man alternating his form quicker and quicker. And his chase becoming faster and faster. Like someone pushed the fast forward button on an eighties video player.

This dream would play out in my mind until I could take no more.

Sitting bolt right up in my bed, I was sure my chilling screams must have been loud enough to wake the whole house. The room still rumbled with the horror of it all as I began to sob.

My terror dreams would plague me on repeated nights during this distressing time. Sympathetic to my terror, my aunts would run to comfort me.

When I wasn't dreaming of the fat or skinny men, I was dreaming of the river.

In this terror video, I'd be standing on the riverbank admiring the fast-flowing water, my thoughts in a panic.

Hadn't my grandmother repeatedly warned me to stay away from there? And hadn't she tried to drown our dog in a weighted bag and thrown her in the river? Then, she'd beaten her with the axe.

Maybe I'd be next?

The river was exciting and the lure for me was too strong. I'd just have a look along the top of the bank, and not by the water's edge. I'd be safe there.

But I was clumsy and tripped. My fall (always in slow motion) had me grabbing desperately for a tuft of grass, a tree branch. Anything. But there was nothing but dirt and leaf matter. I yelled for help as I fell into the water. But no-one was there to save me.

The river was a torrent. It moved at a rapid speed.

As I entered with a splash, the water filled my mouth and nose. The current pulled me along and under the brown murky water. I let out a scream and I gasped for my last breath. I was going to drown…

Grandma's attitude and her lack of empathy exacerbated my anxiety. Perhaps life and survival had hardened her. Perhaps she hadn't always been like this.

***

THE HIGHLANDS

We landed in a bush setting in the highlands near the township of Seymour.

Bruce, looking for work, had started shearing for the farmer who owned the house we were staying in.

Our house stood high on a hill with a long steep track to the road at the bottom. An empty white weatherboard with pine board floors.

We had not a stick of furniture. Only a couple of double beds that came with the house. Nothing more than shearers' quarters I suspect.

We three girls shared a bed together and Bruce and May shared the other.

With no table and chairs, my sisters and I would pretend we were picnicking in the forest. Laying down a rug on the floor and sitting cross-legged to eat any meal. Bruce and May sat on the two wooden crates scrounged from the laundry outbuilding that was to the side of the house. We ate our meals from plates on our laps.

We had no television or radio, just a little record player and a collection of 45s and Mother owned a few albums; a Pat

Boone, Peter Paul and Mary, and the Seekers. Possibly a few more but they are the ones that come to mind.

I loved music and it was the one thing that brought all of us joy. Singing Gypsy Rover, Five Hundred Miles, and Cotton Fields at the top of our voices. It seemed May had a theme going on. Quite a parallel to our own lives at the time.

Bruce would always read us bedtime stories, something our father had never done, exaggerating the fairy-tales and adding his own spin on it. We would listen intently and laugh at his silliness. Perhaps we filled the void of the loss of his two daughters, who now lived with their mother in Melbourne. We thought he was pretty good at fathering duties.

For the first time in ages, peace filled me. My bad dreams had ceased to bedevil me, and I could at last be free. Dancing to the records and playing in the hills mended my troubled mind. If only it could have lasted.

Our toys had not arrived. We had all helped pack them into a wooden tea chest. One with big black lettering stamped all over it, and metal strips to hold it together.

My sisters and I had been allowed to bring our favourite dolls and teddies, but everything else had been packed to arrive on the train. I had tried to be patient, but it had been weeks and still no sign of them.

The truth is they never came. Had Mother put them on the train? Or was this a lie to conceal that she had in fact given them away to some charity organisation or dumped them in the garbage, perhaps. Maybe it was the delivery fee she couldn't afford. Whatever it was, I grieved my toys for ages. Maybe it was my only link to my previous life that really upset me. I'm not sure. But I think the lie perhaps made it worse.

So, I played at make believe. I could be a princess with gum-nut jewels and bottle top coins. And my sisters could be my servants, getting me anything I needed. Or I could play teacher with pebbles for chalk and rocks for blackboards. Presenting lessons in an open-air classroom to my enthusiastic pupils.

That summer I ran free with the wind in my hair, and the sun on my face. Climbing through farm fencing and roaming the paddocks. It was peaceful and I was happy to be away from the arguments and problems that had plagued my family. I could explore the world and just enjoy being a child.

Our family had no fridge, so the cold stores *(when we had any)* were placed in the nearby river. "Nature's fridge" my mother called it. Her experience of living by the Edward proved an advantage. She regularly stocked up on canned food, packaged items, and vegetable produce to make things easier to store.

In the beginning we managed well for food, with Bruce bringing home potatoes and lamb from the farmer.

They had both saved a little money over the last couple of months. In particular, May was cashed up after having sold her old green Holden, only days before our departure from Deniliquin.

But it wasn't long before our happiness started to turn to misery.

I'm not sure if Bruce was paying most of his wages to support his daughters, or if his money just didn't go around among the five of us. Maybe he was gambling it. Or withholding it and stashing it away. Whatever it was, we were running out of money fast.

And our knight's armour wasn't shining as brightly.

***

STARTING SCHOOL

'I've enrolled you into that little school we visited last week. The bus drives straight past our gate. You can walk yourself down and get on if I'm sleeping in,' May told Robyn. May was looking forward to having a break from her eldest. She thought she might cope better with only two kids at home. Robyn was always bored and drove her crazy at times. She'd harped on about school for weeks now.

'You start tomorrow. So, you'll have to be ready by 8.30 to catch the bus. I'll walk down with you tomorrow morning. After that you'll know what to do,' she told her. 'It'll be nice for you to have some new friends. And your teacher seems very nice, don't you think?'

Robyn looked at her *seemingly unimpressed.* 'I don't want new friends! I like my old friends! And where's Dad?' she blurted out all at once. 'I'm hungry! What's for dinner?'

May sighed. Robyn was always difficult. She could be a real little bitch at times. And hadn't May called her that straight to her face. She felt a little guilty as she reflected. But hey, she was only human after all.

'They're in Deniliquin. You know that. And we are here, so there's nothing we can do about that right now.'

'What's for dinner? I hope it's not potatoes again.' Robyn stamped her foot and scowled, not taking a bit of notice of what May just said.

'I don't know yet.' That's the only answer May could give her. She always worried about dinner time. Some nights there was barely anything.

'Bruce is okay, but he's not like Dad.' Robyn sneered as took off out the door in a huff.

May sighed. *Yep, school would be good for both of them.*

Next morning, they made good time, and Robyn left on the bus just after eight thirty.

Finally, she could get a little rest from Robyn's badgering. There were times, frankly, where she had wanted to strangle her.

She worked at the cleaning the house while the little ones played. Popping the Seekers record on, she sang to the music. Washing the dishes and stripping the beds, she sang the chorus repeatedly. She returned to the player over and over to lift the arm and place it on her favourite track.

She blamed herself. *Maybe the separation from her father had brought on Robyn's bad behaviour.* May wasn't sure. But she hoped that Robyn attending school would make a big difference.

Over the next couple of weeks, her daughter seemed happier. And Robyn's absence from the house certainly improved her own situation, but she hadn't expected that Linda would miss Robyn so much.

Instead of Robyn harping at her and driving her mad, it was Linda's crying and sobbing for her sister that frustrated her. How could she have known that this was going to happen? She couldn't stand it.

She said to Linda, 'If the school will take you, I will send you next week with Robyn.'

The following day, she rang from a phone box in town. Linda would join Robyn. And a week later, May was waving them both off. May figured Linda would be fine as she was a bright little child for four. And besides she was turning five in less than two months.

And she could finally have some peace and quiet.

***

A HIGHLAND CHRISTMAS

Mother constantly got us to collect firewood during our play for the stove. We didn't mind. We made it a game. We'd be the three pigs. The pig that built his house of sticks. *Better grab heaps. It takes lots to build a house.*

There were plenty of gum twigs from the gum trees around near the house. Some with ribbons of bark encased with webs and baby spiders.

I'd start screaming loudly whenever I saw any. Robyn wasn't too bothered, however. Routinely squishing their innards by knocking the stick against the trunks of the trees or stomping on them, seemed all part of the process to her.

One morning, Mother came with us and led us further from the house. 'Girls, come on, let's look for a gum branch for a Christmas Tree.'

We couldn't afford a pine tree for the traditional English-look Christmas. But there was plenty of promise in decorating an indigenous species for an Australian one.

We hunted around for ages, looking for a suitable specimen. It needed to have adequate proportions and lots of gum leaves still attached for a good look.

When our prize was chosen, we dragged it home along the smoothest path available across the paddocks mindful to avoid snagging the branch on rocks or large grass tufts.

That afternoon Mother helped us paint our branch. And when it was finished, we all stood back to admire our silver masterpiece, with its shining long eucalyptus leaves and its decorative gum-nuts. It was stunning.

The Highlands school was having a Christmas play. Robyn and I were cast as fairies. Mother made us fairy wings from stockings and skirts of tulle. We held little silver painted wands with a star on the top.

The night of the performance, Bruce sat in the audience, with my mother beside him and Rhonda nursed on her lap. They had wanted to get a good view so had chosen the second row, off centre. It was a magical moment for me, as I sang at the top of my voice, and flapped my fairy wings as I danced on stage in unison with the rest of the children.

I could see my family clapping with the crowd, as the class finished the final Christmas song. Everyone appeared to be entertained by our performance and proud of their little "highland" fairies.

Robyn went to Melbourne with Bruce's family for Christmas while I stayed home with Mother and Rhonda. Santa never made it to the highlands that year. He was only going to Melbourne.

Christmas Eve came and went in that white weatherboard with the silver bush Christmas tree. And Rhonda and I didn't get any presents. But we were young, so we really didn't miss the celebration that much. Or so the story goes.

***

WET BEDS AND WASHING

Our bed was wet again, which wasn't comfortable at all. Especially now the summer had finished, and the cooler mornings were here. Everyone blamed each other for the deed, but truth is it was probably all of us. Mother was mad; she didn't want to wash more pissy sheets.

She chastised us and demanded to know why we hadn't got up to the toilet.

Was she serious? Our toilet was a hellhole.

The toilet was in the outhouse, a short distance from the back door and normally referred to as the Dunny.

Its real purpose though was to accommodate the hundreds of flies and dangerous Arachnids that resided there. A pit of rotting faeces and festering toxic urine gas that bubbled in the bottom of the ground, threatened to asphyxiate any human visitor who entered.

The Redbacks and Huntsmen seemed to be really thriving in there with such an abundance of food, growing monstrous in the poisonous environment.

A wooden box sat atop the hole, to balance your bum, but mine was small. What if I fell in? I'd surely drown in all that bog waste.

The sound of flies buzzing would fill my ears on entry. Their excitement obvious as they feasted on the decay in that cesspool. Female blowflies laid white-fleshed maggots in the shit. An extra delicious meal for the spiders.

Consequently, the dunny was a hurried affair. Spending as little time as possible in that horrible confined fetid space, I made sure my radar stayed on high alert. My terrified eyes stayed glued to the spiders in the corners of the room. I was always tense and ready to run, if they dared even stretch a leg.

It was tough— real tough during daylight hours. I had no chance at night.

Mother wasn't interested in our excuses about being scared of going to the toilet. 'Take those sheets to the wash house,' she said, handing Robyn and me a sheet each.

The smell of the urine really permeated my nostrils. 'It stinks. It's wet,' I said screwing up my face.

Ignoring my complaints, Mother led us out into the freezing early morning conditions with our smelly bundles. The laundry was a wooden outbuilding with dirty worn wooden floors scattered with dried gum leaves that had blown in on the wind. Its plank-board dingy exterior was on a par with the dunny.

The cement troughs, branded with a name I couldn't read, stood centre of the room on the back wall. The rest of the space was bare except for an old kitchen chair, a small wooden footstool— barely off the ground, and a metal bucket with a few old rags thrown over the edges. Mother owned no washing appliances, so it was all hand-washing and hard work.

The primitive clothesline stood at the back of the building a little way to the left. Its wooden poles jammed in the ground when the house was first built. Adjustable sticks were attached to the wire so it could be lifted up or down for height.

Robyn was still pulling faces and protesting her innocence. A better actress than me, she was good at trying to get out of a task. And would have been happy for me to do it alone. Mother wasn't having any of it, however, and handed me the Velvet soap. 'Robyn, help your sister. I've gotta get some hot water from the house. Stay here. I'll be back.'

She cleared off while I pulled the wooden chair close to the trough. I threw the soap on top of the dirty wash pile scrunched in the trough and waited for her return.

She showed up just long enough to turn the tap on over the sheets and add her bucket of hot water. 'It's all yours now,' she said. And walked off towards the house.

I cringed as I placed my hands in the water. It wasn't pleasantly warm as I'd thought it might be, the hot splash barely taking the chill off the ice-cold tank water. I couldn't feel my hands as I plunged them deeper into the frigid contents. *Brrr... it was cold out here.* I shivered as I tried to work out how to wash sheets. I dabbed some soap against the yellow piddle stain I could see bobbing in the water.

'Not like that!' my sister told me. 'You've got to rub the soap up and down like Mum does.' She climbed up onto the footstool beside me, trying to demonstrate the method. 'And use that scrubbing brush there!' She pointed to the other trough where she spied the implement.

Grabbing the brush, I pulled it in a backwards forwards motion and created lovely bubbles in the tub. I lifted them high and threw them in the air. Some landing back in the water and floating on the surface.

'Come on! Stop playing, you're too slow. Just let me do it.' Robyn grumbled under her breath. 'You turn the other tap on. And fill that trough up. We have to rinse.'

I could only get the tap to dribbled out a little crooked stream of tank water. I plugged the drain and waited what seemed like ages. Impatient, I turned the tap off. The half-full trough would have to do. Together we dragged the sheets into the freezing clear water.

After a few swirls and a bob up and down, we were satisfied the rinsing process was complete. And pulled the plug.

We left them to drain while we had a game of clap hand. I was still slow, but Robyn had mastered the moves and chanted the verses of *A Sailor Went to Sea, Sea, Sea.* I played along and tried to get the rhythm.

This morning we enjoyed it more than usual as it warmed our freezing digits. As we sang the words our mouths puffed steam. 'I'm smoking.' I giggled.

'Don't be ridiculous,' said Robyn.

Later, after our attempt to lift out the sheets, we realised they were still full of water. "How do we get the water out?" I asked.

Robyn was like a grown up. She knew everything. 'Wring them out like this, she said, twisting them with both hands. 'Come on, help!'

I squeezed them like she showed me, trying so hard my knuckles turned white and my small hands were freezing again.

Pools of water seeped out and ran into the drain. Its pipe started talking a foreign language— glug glug gurgle thhhhh. Repeating it again, just in case we'd missed it the first time.

Removing them out from their watery vessel proved difficult, and the sheets landed with a thump on the dirty wooden floor. We figured it didn't matter, at least the smell had vanished.

With the bed linen dripping water down our thighs, we headed for the line. Together, we draped them over the wire in a bunched heap. Any attempt to straighten them risked them falling onto the ground below, so we just jammed in a few pegs that were in the tin under the line. And raced off to tell Mother we had finished.

She headed out to straighten them and raised the poles. And those sheets flapped away happily for the rest of the day.

And did we wet the bed again? Yep. I'm afraid to say we did.

***

HAPPY MUMMY

May was addicted to Valium. It was known as the Happy Mummy Pill. The doctors had freely prescribed it to her to treat her depression.

May was starving and her children were hungry. They constantly cried and whined for food. She tried to comfort them, but she was weak and hungry too. She seemed to have taken to yelling at them instead. It didn't seem to matter what she did in her life, it always turned to misery. Perhaps they would all die up here in the mountains.

Maybe we should have stayed at Mum's, even if we clashed at times. At least the children could eat. She loved him, she really did. He was a good man, but he never seemed to have any money. She had been trying to get a little assistance from the government, but that had been a long, drawn-out process. And Cyril certainly didn't want to contribute anything at this stage.

She had tried to contact him for child support, but he was still angry at her and had refused to send anything. She'd even resorting to begging him for money. Explaining that their children were starving made no difference. He seemed to take no pity on any of them.

Bruce was trying so hard, but all the travelling to Melbourne to see his daughters was costing in fuel. And how much of his earnings were going to support them? It seemed he had very little left for his new family.

Any money she'd saved had been spent. For weeks they had had very little left for food. Bruce got a feed with the shearers once a day, which enabled him to work. He'd bring home anything he could that was left over, but today there was nothing left except a jar of Vegemite to stir in some water for a broth. Not very filling but still warm and comforting.

She'd have to sedate the girls and put them to bed early. And tomorrow she might need to rely on the good heartedness of the store owner to run a credit note until she could pay for it. At least the medication helped the girls sleep away their hunger. They all risked starvation. She felt helpless, shameful, and entirely to blame.

It upset her when she lay down at night and thought about the all her hardships. She tried hard to focus on the future. But the future wasn't looking good at the moment. Her mind constantly tortured her. Maybe, she was all those things her voices were saying she was.

Some days, her life was just not worth getting up for. She preferred to stay in bed and only get out for short periods to check on the girls. They were good at amusing themselves, spending hours drawing and colouring in. On a bad day, it was easier for her to stay drugged in a zombie-like state. Nothing bothered her then.

At other times when she was in a happy mood, engaging with her children was wonderful. They would laugh and dance to the music on her record player and sing the lyrics together. With her Happy Mummy Pill, May could choose when she wanted to participate in life, and when she didn't.

***

STARVING

It was bitterly cold. The fog had not lifted in the highlands today and the sun hid behind the blanket of cloud.

I huddled inside with my family. Blankets had been pulled from the beds and wrapped around our bodies for warmth.

None of us had ventured out to collect the wood. The weather hampered any effort to see even a few feet in front of us. Besides, mother knew the twigs would be soaked and impossible to light.

The last of the small logs left on the hearth had been used during the early afternoon. Even though Mother had tried to skimp on them and use them sparingly, they had still run out.

The living area had cooled off considerably. *I wished Bruce was here to bring home some sticks.* But that wasn't going to be happening, as Bruce had gone up north somewhere. All I knew was he was shearing.

'No good hanging around the highlands,' he'd said. 'All the sheep here need their jumpers on this time of the year.'

I knew what he meant. I could feel the highland chill drilling into my bones like tooth pain. My skeletal muscle stiff from lack of movement and heat. I felt locked in a comatose freeze mode, lying about on our timber floor snuggled with my sisters. We shared a pillow among three, none of us even bothering to fight for ownership of it today.

We were drifting in and out of sleep today. (*Perhaps May had dosed us to avoid our suffering*) I had lost a lot of weight and with almost no body fat, I was really feeling the cold.

My teeth were clanging, and an uncontrolled shivering of my starving body was the only way to keep it warm.

My sisters and I would be in bed early tonight. I couldn't wait. Back to back we'd be warm as we slept.

It was unbearable up here in the mountains— coldness like I had never known before. I found it hard to imagine lasting through the relentless winter here.

I became homesick for the heat and the skies of New South Wales. Even in the cold season, when Jack Frost got your toes, the afternoon sky was vivid blue and cheerful.

Victorian skies resembled dirty cotton. The clouds blocking out any sun, warmth or cheer.

High above the fluff was a ruddy shade of grey-blue but only visible for short periods of the day. Any bright blue sky was a rarity to be worshipped. The insipid cloud cover never parted unless the winds blew up and carried them away.

My mood became grey to match the weather. Plus, starving and trapped on an isolated mountain— no wonder my mother was depressed and couldn't function. Like exiled Russians in Siberia, we almost died locked up in those extreme conditions.

I craved the yellow sun to warm my body and tint my skin, willing the misery to end, because I could stand it no longer.

But then what if the grey was the coming out of the darkness. Out of the nightmare.

And perhaps the dirty cotton wool clouds were the angels trying to penetrate the grey, so they could watch us children and keep us safe. We did survive that cold, miserable winter, and for that I was grateful.

From a young age, my sisters and I were very skilled at looking after ourselves. Getting something to eat was something we learned pretty quickly. Often food was scarce, so we learned to share and make do with whatever was available. Many times, we'd scavenge fruit from old orchard trees or pick berries that grew wild. One thing my mother learnt from Grandma was survival.

In our crowded bed at night, we could forget about food. *(Just like, "Three in a bed and the middle one said..."* Robyn always chose the middle. We created a game called "Tickles on Backs". It would soothe us and curb our hunger.

The pain of starvation eating at my insides came in waves. Rumbling noises echoing in hollow space. Twisting, torturing pain in my intestines. The thought of food, always there, consuming my every waking hour.

We'd lie side by side and draw on each other's back with our fingers. We often duped Rhonda into tickling Robyn for longer. She couldn't tell the passing of time because she was still young and innocent.

We'd tickle great masterpieces of the Australian bush, like the rivers and gum of the Edward. Or drawings of ballerinas in tutus and shoes that laced and crisscrossed up their legs.

We drew dogs that lived in kennels, cats that climbed up trees and two storey mansions on hills with white picket fences and cottage flower gardens to die for.

After a bit, it would be my turn to roll over to receive the tickle. It would calm me and send me quickly to sleep. *Or maybe it was the Valium. I am not sure.*

I only realised much later that my eldest sister's demand for the middle position ensured she always had two goes to our one.

***

SLEEPING SOUNDLY

May made mistakes. She had not been given a manual on how to tackle every situation when it came to raising children. And if she had one, would it have made a difference? Probably not. As the manual wouldn't have covered, *how to stop your children from starving.*

Having escaped her life of violence, she found a new determination. She was going to be a better mother than Antoinette. Wasn't she always telling her children how much she loved them? Unlike her own mother, who was constantly comparing everyone else's to her own.

Antoinette found it hard to embrace her children. Years of circumstance had made her hard. She saw her children as an asset to help her make money, instead of a blessing from God to be cherished and nurtured. Her life struggle impacted on her time spent with them.

May wanted her new life to work. She really did. But she could see that her plans were not materialising.

How had it come to this? Only today Robyn had questioned her about her attendance at school.

That child of hers was a bit too smart for her own good. May had been dumbfounded at her questions. She was worried now.

Bruce didn't know what she'd done. She had rung him from the phone box in Seymour the other day. Told him they were fine. But could he send them some money because they were getting low on food. *(In actual fact they were more than low.)*

He'd left her some money but not nearly enough. He'd been expecting to finish up north last week. But it had been a good year for shearing and he still had at least another 3 weeks of work left to do.

She was sure he would have been very angry at her, but they were her children and it tortured her watching them begging for food, withering away. She'd only meant to put them to sleep for the night, but they had slept longer than expected. And then she'd kept them home the following day to make sure they'd have no side effects.

In the afternoon she walked them up the mountain to town. A probably still-woozy Robyn wouldn't stop whinging for a drink all the way. May had lost it with her, called her a little bitch and dragged her down by the stream and dunked her head in it. "You want a drink! Here drink!" she'd said.

Getting up from kneeling by the water, May had wanted to die. The guilt enveloped her. How could she? She was the same as all the rest of them, treating her child like that.

Robyn, wet and sobbing, continued the in silence. As did May. The week had been too much. Maybe she wasn't well herself, as she hadn't eaten today. She needed to buy some food for them before they all died.

In town, the storekeeper had taken pity on them and had credited some supplies to feed them. It was embarrassing to ask for help and each time she did, it wore away at May's self-worth. But really, what choice did she have? It was that or starve.

And she was worried sick she'd be found out. Robyn's school friends and her teacher had enquired about her absence. Robyn had no recollection of her time off school and questions and suspicion were circulating.

She'd had bouts of depression lately and May had been trying to hide the fact from Bruce. Thankfully, he hadn't seen the goings on. But he'd be back in a few weeks. Hopefully her talk with the teacher today would sort out the misunderstanding before he found out.

May cast her eyes upwards, but not directly at the teacher. Hopefully she could explain the girls' absence. 'Robyn and Linda have been in bed with high fevers,' she told Miss Prime.

'That must be why Robyn's memory failed her,' the teacher said.

May nodded.

'Must be some childhood virus the girls picked up,' Miss Prime said.

May shrugged. 'No, they never had a rash.'

May was feeling jittery, she hoped like hell the teacher believed her lie. Again, she shrugged. 'Yes, I probably should have rung the school, but we don't have a phone. And Bruce had the car, so there was nothing I could do about it.' She bobbed her head up and down. 'I am sorry. Yes, they are well now, thankfully.'

After their discussion, the teacher and May both exchanged smiles. But May could see that the teacher was still mulling it around in her head. May didn't want her children taken from her. She hoped she'd been convincing.

***

BATHING IN THE ELEMENTS

We had been bathing in the house because I remember that Rhonda had repeatedly been told to stop slurping water that accumulated in the dirty plug. A habit that annoyed everyone.

Either we had run out of tank water or something had stopped working in the house, for May had started taking us to the dam over near the shearing sheds for an early morning douse.

It was spring and we had managed to survive the winter.

It was a bit of a walk to the dam and the mornings in the highlands were still freezing cold.

The shearers had packed up all their belongings and moved on to new sheds. So, there was no-one around to spy us. It was quite early, and the sun had not been up for long. Even the birds were still nesting their young. They weren't going scavenging until the fog lifted a bit.

They must have been laughing at us. *Look at those silly humans moving out along the hills at such an ungodly hour in such arctic conditions.*

Mother instructed us to strip off our pyjamas and hop in the dam.

So, I stood shivering by the side of the muddy water, its colour reminding me of the Edward. But that was the only resemblance. It definitely wasn't very big and nowhere near as pretty as my grandmother's river. There wasn't even a tree around.

It was not a pleasant activity on this still fresh morning. And it certainly was no-one's first choice for bathing.

But having shared a wet bed together, the other alternative was to smell like piss for the day. Which probably wouldn't be pleasant for anyone at school.

So, making my way to the edge, I tip-toed over the dewy grass to where the mudline met the water.

My sisters were squealing in unison with me as we entered the freezing pool.

We went in only on the bank edge as deep as our knees. Mother told us to squat down to wash our private bits. 'Use the soap,' she called out from the rim. We had been given a rag and a bar of soap and Robyn had washed first before handing it to me.

I could not stand the cold. So, I splashed the water onto my naked body and washed that way.

Lathering up the cloth and scrubbing my skin, I rinsed again with the slashes of iced mud water. I wondered, *Am I really any cleaner?*

Rhonda sat near the edge in the shallows. Sailing past her, eager to get dried off, I suggested she stand up and wash. Flinging the soap and cloth to her, I raced up to grab a towel. I dried myself quickly and threw on my day clothes.

Mother tried to hurry her up. Rhonda wasn't good at hurrying and it was a source of frustration for me. I liked to be organised and on time. Not Rhonda. She seemed to have all day.

'Hurry up, Rhonda, or we will leave you here in the dam with mud in your crack.' I couldn't help taunting her. She poked out her tongue, and Mother told me to leave her alone.

'I'm coming now.' Rhonda pouted, and pulled a face at me.

'If the wind changes, you'll stay like that,' Mother said.

It was one of her old wives' tales, but at age five, I think I really believed it.

After a quick dry off with the help of May, Rhonda headed off home with the rest of us, to scrounge for something to eat for breakfast.

On weekends, we'd trek across the paddocks to the river. Mother demonstrated how to beat a stick in front of us, on the ground, to scare away snakes. We were confident and beat our sticks with validity.

Approaching the river, we could hear the mountain water long before we saw it. Its power echoed through the air. The smell of the sweet damp vegetation was our beacon to navigate. And every time you'd arrive and spy its wild beauty, it slapped you, taking your breath and threatening to floor you. So different from the Edward. Its crystal-clear water was all bubble and foam.

Like primitive natives, we'd skinny dipped in its shallows, all of us enjoying its magic aura, but gasping and jiggling at its frigid liquid. We danced from one foot to another, trying to warm ourselves as we washed. Never-ending torrents of fizzy water cascaded over the rocks like a fall.

We strewed our towels out on surrounding granite rocks, letting them absorb any warmth still present inside from yesterday's sun. The bar of soap shared between us created more reason for arguments.

***

A CAR ACCIDENT

Bruce drove us in the Humber. He loved to sit Rhonda on his knee and let her steer. A silly childish prank, that delighted a child of three. 'See, you can drive.' He enjoyed teasing her.

Bruce was always goofing around. A bit of a character, he made our mother smile. She was happy whenever he was around. And we liked him too.

One day, Rhonda was beside him in the middle of front seat, which was her favourite spot when not on his knee.

How we ended up in a smash is unclear to me, but with big sprung bench seats and no seat belts, we all bounced around quite a bit.

Like a fairground dodgem attraction, I was jerked forward with force. The bumper ploughed through the saplings and came to rest amongst the trees on the roadside verge.

There was silence for a brief moment, as the air around me radiated outward and then back. Like an invisible force, it smacked into me like a flick of elastic, and brought me back to the moment.

I could hear Rhonda screaming and it made me feel lightheaded. I swallowed hard in an attempt to compose myself. But I started shaking.

In my confused state, all I could see was the back of Rhonda's head from my thrashed position in the back seat. I couldn't see her face or the front of her body.

Nausea roiled through me and I tried to escape through the back door.

After rattling the handle, it opened with a groan, and I scrambled out relatively unscathed. My sister Robyn following close behind.

The vehicle had come to an abrupt stop. And everyone sitting in the front had been thrown against the dashboard.

Rhonda was making such a ruckus.

With mother unable to console as her, she nudged the door open.

Blood smeared Rhonda's face and any attempt to wipe her tears meant spreading the blood further. It was plain to see its source lay in the nasal region, where a small stream trickled.

Mother, on the other hand, appeared to be uninjured except for a complaint about her neck being a little sore, as she rubbed against it with her right hand, moving her head backwards and forwards.

Rhonda had hit her nose down on the dashboard and had then been flung back into the seat. She'd been screaming, but May had settled her to sobs instead. 'Help us out,' Mother said to Robyn.

I had started crying and my anxiety was making me feel faint. Robyn hated blood too, so she wasn't any good at helping with a bleeding accident victim any more than I was. So, it was left to May to carry her out alone.

While we sat on the ground like she'd told us to, she brought Rhonda to join us.

Bruce was still in the vehicle and May headed back towards the battered shell.

As she approached, he slid out from the driver's side, holding one hand to his bloodied head. The other gripping his shirt across his chest.

His injuries looked serious. His body had been rammed against the steering wheel, and his head had hit the windscreen, smashing the glass, and embedding fragments into his skull.

As he left the vehicle, Bruce battled to keep upright, and he stumbled only a few steps before draping his top half over the bonnet.

Shards of glass that he'd pulled from his forehead, lay on the ground. He'd taken his handkerchief from his pocket and pressed it hard across his brow to stem the bleed. Bruce was in real danger of passing out.

His complaints of a headache had Mother leaning over him to assess his condition. He stayed slumped over the car for some minutes before making his way over to where we sat. Mother walked him slowly over and they joined us on the ground. Unable to sit, Bruce sprawled prone beside us, moaning.

I was traumatised and the blood covering his hands and face made me nauseous.

Nobody talked and all was silent, except for the occasional light snore coming from Rhonda as she slept. Exhausted and in shock from her battering, she had closed her eyes and drifted into a fitful sleep. And Bruce moaned as he tried to come to terms with his pain.

Later, I realised I had slept too. For how long I wasn't sure. But my need to pee woke me. Rubbing my dirty hands across my eyes, I stretched and instantly felt my muscles pull. They had certainly taken some of the impact.

I didn't dwell on it however, as urgency took precedence and I headed for a suitable tree.

The road's isolation meant we had not encountered any passing traffic. So, when everyone felt able, Mother decided that we would walk in the direction of home.

Like wounded zombies in a horror movie, bloodied and injured, we stumbled back to our house. Resting as we needed. And taking turns to piggy-back.

With no telephone and no money to pay, we didn't consult the doctors. Every family member patched-up as best as possible.

May's reluctance to see a doctor stemmed from the fact that Rhonda had had a previous head injury the year before in Deniliquin. And she felt she would surely be scrutinised for the cause. The real tragedy however was that Rhonda was now in real danger of permanent damage.

I'd carried the guilt for some time. The narrative of the story went, "You hit your sister over the head with a wooden toy train. It was an accident. You were just swinging it about."

Funny thing was I had no recollection of a deed. A deed I'm sure I would have been severely chastised for. Maybe I was just too small. But its repeated mentions felt like brain washing. Rehearsed perhaps. Something about it didn't quite fit. But I still carried the guilt.

Rhonda had spent months in a wooden playpen to mend her injury last time. This time she would just rest at home. Yes, she'd be okay.

They towed the vehicle to a workshop, and when it was finally repaired, we left the highlands behind.

***

FIVE BECOMES FOUR

Since the car accident, Bruce had become argumentative and suffered terrible headaches. His erratic moods worried May. His decision to leave Victoria and move May's family to Moree in New South Wales seemed a little impulsive to her. But maybe the sunshine would improve everyone's health.

Rhonda didn't seem to be any worse for wear and had recovered well. *Thank goodness!* May had been worried for weeks that her daughter should have been taken to the hospital. Thankfully her nose didn't appear to have been broken and the black around her eyes had all but disappeared.

Moree was a working town of cotton growers and grain farmers. And it was where travelling shearers like Bruce found employment. She was happy to be able to rent a small caravan in the local park. During the busy peak times, accommodation was scarce and expensive so a caravan was all they could afford.

She wasn't sure how they would all go in a hot and stuffy van. Adjusting to gypsy life was going to be a little difficult. But May was optimistic and very relieved to finally have an income coming in.

The shopping precinct was close by which was a bonus. At least we girls could walk happily with her and not complain of tired legs like we had in the Highlands.

Bruce had always taken the car whenever he chased a job with the shearing mob. So many times, they had been forced to trudge miles in the highlands to get into town during his absence. Here in Moree it didn't matter as everything was so close. Linda would enjoy the convenience.

Gone was the peace and quiet of the countryside, replaced instead with noise and bustle. Here seasonal workers and struggling families crowded the park.

Everything felt alien. She could have been in a third world country the way the heat radiated off the tin walls. She felt like a refugee family living in makeshift housing.

Her neighbour's accommodation was so close, she could hear their chatter, sounding like a foreign language as it entwined itself with others in the park. The babble jumbled together. Only hearing snippets of conversation at a time.

The showers and toilets were a busy shared affair where line ups were common. The idle chatter became relentless. So much so, that some nights she took to washing from a bucket and sending her girls to line up alone with the other females, preferring to miss the stampede herself at peak times.

Her man had started work in the shearing sheds and brought home a good wage. But his migraine headaches became more frequent and she was worried sick about the way he would bang his head on the walls of the van most evenings.

It was hard to watch. Her knight that had come to her rescue was injured and unrecognisable. His mood swings were distressing for all, and their love was struggling.

He was miserable.

May's suggestion for him to see the doctor fell on deaf ears after the local GP had failed to diagnose anything on a previous visit when they had first arrived in town. She could do nothing more to help him.

Then one day, suddenly he was gone. Just like he could stand no more.

At first, she was puzzled at his disappearance and she worried that he may have ended it all.

She was so sad, she cried day and night. It was one of the most intense shattering times of her life. The impact of her disappointment and sorrow coloured all of them black. Her daughters did not understand his decision either.

She rang his family in case he had harmed himself and trolled the streets and talked to other workers in the park. No-one knew his whereabouts. It seemed he had just disappeared.

His cowardly departure created a bombardment of emotion for her. The voices in her head laughed at her stupidity. *He couldn't possibly love you. No one ever had.*

'Maybe he'll come back,' she told her children. And she waited and waited, until it became apparent that he wouldn't return.

In the days that followed, she came to terms with the fact that she was not to blame. And it was then that the voices in her head disappeared.

She was now alone with her children. Alone and destitute. She would have to leave Moree but had no idea where they would go.

May never saw or heard from Bruce again. Having tried to find him for years to no avail, she eventually had to lay that relationship to rest forever.

***

MELBOURNE CITY

We stayed in Footscray with Uncle Frank. His house an old single storey terrace jammed in amongst the other Victorian cottages. I'm not sure how long we stayed, just long enough to pick up the pieces and move on again.

I wanted to stay, not that I voiced it. It was just what I felt. I loved the city and would have been happy somewhere in one of those little houses close by.

While Frank was working, Mother would take us exploring. We'd walk the Queen Victoria Market till our legs felt like they'd fall off.

It was like a big sale yard, with its roofed shed pavilions full of traders lined in rows— sellers of colourful imported Asian clothing in tiny sizes; clockwork toys; men's wrist watches; lace tablecloths; junk jewellery; pets; flowers and food to go. You could buy everything you needed at the market, all at a good price.

But while Mother hung around the produce stalls, her budget loaned from Frank did not stretch to allow for extra wares. A messy noisy place, it had an overpowering smell of sulphur radiating off the cruciferous vegetables. It was not so much the boxes of packed greens but the squished vegetation that lay on the floor that created the stench, which made it both nauseating and uncomfortable. I found it hard not to gag and always couldn't wait to leave.

Stall holders adorned with aprons and pencils tucked behind their ears would weigh your purchase. Retrieving a note pad from their pocket, they did the math. A thank you and an exchange of money and we'd be on our way.

Mother carried a basket and added some apples to the mix. I hated apples. She'd buy oranges too as they were Robyn's favourite. But oranges were cumbersome to peel, and their juice dripped down my face and all over my fingers. I liked apricots and prune plums. Grandma grew them out on the farm. Mother didn't buy them for me, so I never ate much fruit.

If you hated crowds, then this was not the place for you. It could be shoulder to shoulder people most days. Lots of foreign faces, exotic languages and relentless noise.

Vendors spruiked a deal with the bargain hunter. Mothers chastised their children for not sticking together. Boxes made scraping noises as stallholders pushed them around on the ground. Clanging, banging, humming, squealing. So much stimulation. It was perfect for me.

We'd take a tram and head for the city. There we'd window shop and stroll the departments stores, their big window displays enticing us to enter.

European fashion draped on headless mannequins, and some torsos with just the stub of the humerus, the rest of the appendage amputated. Many had thin anorexic figures, with faces caked in exaggerated eye makeup and pumped-up lips of red. Their hair consisted of glossy nylon strands of different colours, styled into bob curls or beehive ponytails on top of their hard plaster skulls.

Businesses flaunted handbags and wallets of kangaroo fur, handmade belts of tooled leather and exotic crocodile skin. With fancy pressed silver-plate and artisan copper buckles.

Shoe stores sold stilettos and sandals in all colours; knee-high patent boots in a lovely gloss red; pointed toe flats, Mary Jane T-Straps and canvas casuals.

May would try on the shoes, admiring their style. Checking out how good her feet looked in the little foot mirror standing on the floor. 'No thank you, I don't have the money today!' she'd tell the store assistant after the woman had climbed nearly two storeys up a ladder to grab the box on the top shelf.

Myer was a store for the wealthy. We loved to browse its luxury items. 'It costs nothing to look,' May would say. And that was true. We never bought anything, but I'm sure mother envied the snob-nosed women that were lined up at the perfume counter for Madame Rochas or Chanel No.5.

Something she could afford occasionally was a record. Usually a 45. Brashs had all your vinyl music— The Beatles, Elvis Presley, Tom Jones, and Neil Diamond. There was lots of happiness in Brashs.

I enjoyed everything about the city. But the best bit was the ease of travel. Even in the sixties, Melbourne's public transport was good. My favourite mode was the tram.

Swamped with city commuters, riding the trams was always a hurried affair. Negotiating the steep steps was difficult when I was young. I wasn't very tall, and I certainly wasn't fast.

You had to rush to be seated, or else you could be thrown into someone's knees. Maybe that was the attraction. The whole adrenaline rush to get on and grab a seat before someone pushed past you and took the only seat left available.

Kids could stand. After all, *it was polite to let the adults sit.* *"Children should be seen and not heard" was not just every parent's chant. But every other adult's too.* They'd tell us their old wives' tales with an aim to scare us into submission. Where was their punishment for all their mistruths and propaganda? I hated being a child. I couldn't wait to grow up and have no one bossing me around and telling me lies.

***

A DAY ON THE TRAM

May decided she would stay in Melbourne for a while until she got on her feet again. She couldn't go back to Deniliquin. Not yet anyhow. She couldn't tolerate Antoinette's crazy behaviour. It had nearly destroyed her last time and she would not let it happen again.

She liked spending time with the girls. May and the girls. Everyone referred to her family as that. It was like a term of endearment. Her brood. She liked it. There was nothing she loved more in the world than her girls.

She'd often dressed them alike in pretty creations she'd spent hours sewing for them. That had been a while ago. Things hadn't been going great for her for quite some time now. Her thoughts wandered... *If one had been a boy, it wouldn't have been the same. It would have been May and the children. It just didn't have the same ring about it.* Boys weren't her thing anyway. Cyril had wanted one, but she was happy with her girls.

May noticed the tram approaching and yelled, 'Quick, this is it.' She grabbed Rhonda and Linda by the arm as she turned her head in Robyn's direction and ordered her to follow. 'Come on!'

With only a few minutes to board, she scrambled to find a seat that would accommodate them all. Within mere minutes, they were off down the tracks.

'Where's Robyn?' May asked no one in particular. But Robyn was not aboard. 'Shit! where's Robyn? Linda, where is she? Wasn't she behind you?" May flapped her words without taking a breath. Her anxiety rose as she realised Robyn hadn't followed them into the tram.

'Tickets please,' came the call from the Connie. His money satchel opened as he made his way between the seats to issue his coloured paper tickets.

'Tickets please,' he called again as he worked his way towards them.

'We've gotta get off!' she whispered. Her stomach churned, her head spun as she saw the uniform of the conductor a couple of seats away, luckily distracted by one of the commuters.

She didn't want to lose control in front of everyone. Her mind whizzed frantically, conjuring up thoughts that were ridiculous. Realising that time was precious, she leapt to her feet and pulled the cord that ran along the top of the interior, *used to indicate your intended departure at the next stop.*

May could see the tram stop up ahead as she pushed her face to the window. 'Quickly, we're getting off,' she said. Holding her pointer finger against her lips, she hoped the girls would understand the importance of being quiet. If she snuck off now she wouldn't need to purchase a ticket.

Grabbing a hold of the kids' hands, she waited.

As she heard the brake being applied, and the tram gripped the metal rails imbedded into the road, she gathered their belongings. She had to be quick as other passengers were poised, ready to exit out her side door.

She became fixated as she planned her escape.

Anyone standing jerked forward as the tram came to a screeching holt. Holding the top of the seat in front, she steadied her feet.

Some experienced passengers that were used to this sudden interruption to their ride, managed to stay upright and balanced. Many braced for the next sudden movement that would soon follow, when the driver would take off again, and they could continue on their way.

Squeezing her children's hands to check they were still attached, she moved down the steps before anyone could even realise they were gone. As she stepped onto the pavement and into street, she noticed another tram heading her way on the opposite side of the road. If they hurried, they could catch it. Still attached to her children, she navigated them through the traffic and across to the other side, arriving safely with barely moments to spare.

'Get on,' she shouted at them, practically dragging them up by their arms. She wasn't cross, but just wanted to get back down the road to Robyn.

But it was too late. Robyn was not there. Devastated and really scared, panic threatened to overwhelm her. *Did Robyn get on another tram? If so, she could end up anywhere in Melbourne. Did she wander off in the traffic?* Her mind screamed questions at her. *Oh, where is she?*

Rhonda and Linda started to cry. *Oh no! She couldn't deal with them upset as well.* 'Shhh, it's okay.' She tried comforting them, while trying to stay calm herself. *What the hell was she going to do now?*

'Has anyone seen a little girl with blonde hair? About this tall?' She motioned with her hands. 'Very thin build. She was left behind when the tram took off. Not ten minutes ago.' She continued with her description of the clothing her daughter was wearing. She surveyed the surroundings. Scanning the faces of individuals for any indication they knew something. Anything!

There was little response to her pleas, and she was aware that not everyone was paying attention.

'Please anyone!'

Some started shaking their heads no. While others began to speak. "No, we've just arrived." "No! No little girl here." "Oh you poor thing. Hope you find her soon."

Well-meaning people, but their answers and opinions totally useless to May.

'Where's the police station? Can someone tell me.' They pointed in the direction she should go, and gave instructions of how to get there.

She wasted no more time. Grabbing a hold of her daughters again, she headed up the street. Walking as fast as the girls could manage.

As luck would have it, she spied a police officer quite close by. And he was happy to escort them to the city station.

Robyn was there and relief washed over her as she realised the search was over.

'Robyn's been waiting for you to pick her up. She was brought in earlier very upset. She said you left her behind,' said the woman officer eyeing her off suspiciously.

'We've been frantic,' May said. 'She missed the tram. And we've come as soon as we could, officer.' They were going to scrutinise her, she was sure. *Did they think she had abandoned her own daughter?*

'A young lady found her alone and crying. She brought her here to the station. You will need to fill in some paperwork and then she's ready to go, I think.' Mother waited patiently while someone found her a pen. 'Bye Robyn. Keep close to your mum. It was nice meeting you,' the officer along with her colleagues called to her together.

'Bye!' Robyn called out, giving them a smile and a little wave.

The public servant behind the desk asked her a few personal questions and made drilling eye contact at her.

Who does she think she is, anyhow? It was just a misunderstanding, that's all. It isn't my fault.

'Let's go,' said May in a huff, as she took her girls and headed out of the police station. What a day. She just wanted to head back to Footscray. Shopping could wait for another day.

PART THREE: CRIMINALS

LOVE AT FIRST SIGHT

The next phase in my life was dangerous and tragic and full of adventure. We were in for one hell of a ride.

A male came into our lives that caused so much damage, that it would unravel us all. He caused great upheaval and dark days for all of us.

He knocked on the door. Imagine if he hadn't… but he did. And fate is a strange thing.

Melbourne. We were in Melbourne. He came to the door and it was love at first sight. Well that's how the story goes.

May started a relationship with a stranger. I know this is not so unusual and many people do. The problem however was the three of us. He told everyone he was Yugoslavian. With his features so dark and the origin of his name, I'm guessing a Serbian background.

Why was he here in Australia and what was his story? I'm sure he had a chequered past. May should have been more careful, but deception is easy when trust is gained. And May needed to trust in someone.

They talked in private, and my sisters and I were not invited. Between them, they became a couple. He promised her love and stability, so she took it and dragged us children along for the ride.

His cold black eyes cut through you like shards of coal, the whites a stark clash against the iris. He always stared from a distance, as if in a tranced state of thought. You couldn't read him, but you knew something wasn't right.

96

Longer on the top and trimmed at the sides, his hair matched the colour of his eyes. He had a natural olive complexion with a permanent five o'clock shadow, and he chewed his tongue, like some chew tobacco, making a menacing sucking sound.

You never quite knew what he was thinking as he never looked you straight in the eye. Rhonda accepted his presence, enjoying his stories and compliments. On the other hand, Robyn and I could feel his menace. Truth was, we were a little scared of him.

Being a foreigner, he looked quite different from anyone my mother had ever laid eyes on before. Maybe that was the attraction. I would like to think she was cautious, but I know she wasn't.

"Strangers can be dangerous. Never go with them," Mother constantly warned us. Did she even realise this was actually what she did herself? Probably not.

We moved into his modest bungalow, with cement sheet panels of grey. A drab bachelor space, with male paraphernalia and grime. It matched his personality perfectly. Just a shelter or hideout, perhaps. Like an underground bunker where the light couldn't penetrate.

Or was this just my interpretation of my feelings towards him, as my instincts of dread heightened inside my young self.

The unkept yard with long grass and weeds hadn't been mowed for quite some time. An overgrown fenced veggie garden out the back displayed woody plant stems gone to seed. Its decline attributed to its owner having been way in the city working.

He introduced us to his huge striped Tabby. A flea-ridden mongrel that roamed the streets, its affection saved only for him, smooching and meowing in a hoarse vocal display whenever he was near. It only understood Yugoslav commands and showed no interest in us at all.

The Yugoslav had an annoying habit of clearing his throat, chewing his spittle, and then distributing it on the ground.

Possibly a trace of TB or the effects of his cigarette addiction. It was disgusting and even as a child I would cringe.

On his feet, he wore ugly black thongs, casual ethnic style footwear designed for ease and comfort. I don't know why I remember these as part of his attire, but I do. Maybe intimidated by his haunting stare, I spent a lot of time looking down at his feet. I hated them.

He had been working in Melbourne but returned to the Ford factory in Geelong with us, his new ready-made family. May had no money, so I'm sure she jumped at the chance for free accommodation at the Yugoslav's.

Her lover was a master at stealing vegetables or eggs from his neighbours. No wonder the garden out the back was overgrown. Why bother growing them when you could source them from others. And when he felt like chicken, he'd steal them too. They were easy pickings.

He'd bring them home to Mother. And she would pluck them for him in the bath full of water. Gone were her inhibitions and her reluctance to do such a job. I found it disgusting and disturbing. The murder of a chicken, its feathers, guts and blood in the tub where we would later bathe.

We went to the public school behind the back fence and across the road. Rhonda started prep, but she didn't settle in at all. She soon created frustration for her teachers and an annoyance for mother by returning home every chance she got.

But eventually all that didn't matter, as we all packed up a few months later and headed back to Melbourne.

Perhaps the Yugoslav's criminal activity went further than I knew. But we never returned to that dingy grey man cave. And it was erased from my life in an instant.

***

HERE ONE MINUTE, GONE THE NEXT

We moved into an old house in the suburb of Collingwood, with mouse poop scattered inside the cupboards and an infestation of earwigs in the yard. An old run-down weatherboard with the white paint peeling from all the exterior walls. Not a great impression for my seven-year-old eyes.

But mother set about cleaning and making it liveable. She was always good at making our space as much like a home as she could with very little. The vermin had moved in as the house had sat vacant for some time. And they were hard to eradicate completely whilst we stayed.

It was a only a brief stopover again however (a couple of months at most). Just long enough for the Yugoslav to start a new job, for us to attend a new school, get a little puppy, skip paying the rent and utilities and move on.

I likened our life to that of a board game. Roll the dice and take your turn.

You find a house; you are safe. Stay, and miss a turn.

No job, no money, go back one square.

The rent is due. You can't pay. You must leave your house and go back to the start.

If there is money in your purse, you can move forward and have another turn. The pawns move backwards and forwards across the board of life. And the dice always in play.

I lost countless friendships during our nomadic lifestyle. No one would even remember where the new girl and her sisters had gone. Who really cared? *What were their names again?* It became exhausting. In childhood, the best part of your day should be spent playing with friends. But we never had time to make any. I was always the new girl at school. And over the years it never got any easier.

Each time my first day was spent with the teacher parading me in front of the class. I was always on display like a freak show novelty. Their well-meaning attempt at making me feel welcomed, actual managed to exacerbate my anxiety. I would dread it. Instead of allowing me to just anonymously blend into the fabric of the classroom, I was made the centre of attention, which only heightened my sense of fear.

The teacher would always choose a studious peer to accompany me for my transition. She would introduce me to the other class members and show me all the amenities.

Being blessed with auburn curls and green eyes, I was treated like some exotic rare species. Everyone wanted to look and lay claim to having played with this rare specimen.

I met many lovely little girls, for whom I am forever grateful. Most, unfortunately, got lost in my memories forever.

I was apt at dealing with uncomfortable situations and new surroundings, so I would take a deep breath and just get on with it. Not that I liked it. I just didn't have a choice.

My mother's mental health problems were not obvious to me during adolescence. I had known nothing else my entire life, and no-one bothered to tell me.

May showed us love and affection. A humble, friendly woman with simple needs. But she was sick and depressed. Having her soul battered and destroyed during her upbringing certainly damaged her beyond repair. She did not raise her voice often, but that's not to say that she didn't punish us.

Her favourite weapons of arsenal included hairbrushes, wooden spoons *(she broke a few of those)* or the dreaded jug cord. She used them if we stepped out of line, stinging our legs and smarting our buttocks.

The jug cord however soon fizzled out because of its ability to inflict injury.

May did not want to repeat the violence of yesteryear.

***

A PUPPY FOR A DAY

May loved other people's cast-off animals— she accepted strays or injured. She couldn't stand to see them homeless or injured. Perhaps this is how she obtained the little puppy for Rhonda's sixth birthday.

Rhonda still didn't like school and she was having trouble making new friends. With our lives so disrupted, it was no wonder she was having friendship problems.

'Happy Birthday,' we all chanted and sang her the birthday song that morning before we headed off to school. We still didn't have much money, so mother's promise to Rhonda of a surprise later in the afternoon, excited us all. We lived close to the school, so we were able to walk ourselves, while mother got on with her day.

When the home bell rang that afternoon, I hurried to the school gate to meet my sisters for our stroll home.

Robyn and I quizzed Rhonda all the way home about what she thought it might be. She really had no idea and neither did we. All of us guessed a toy of some sort.

'A doll that talks,' said Robyn knowing Rhonda wanted one.

'A pram, or cot. And a new doll,' I suggested.

'Maybe a hundred toys!' said six-year-old Rhonda, excited.

We all loved birthdays. Mother normally gave us something extravagant, if she could. *But I knew she wasn't going to get one hundred toys.*

Arriving home, we scurried to the old timber front door and knocked. *(With its panels chipped and marked, it really could use a lick of paint.)* Gathered on the small cement porch, we called out impatiently to Mother, 'Open up.'

As the door opened, I could hear little whimpering noises coming from somewhere. 'Rhonda, go look out the back. Your surprise is out there,' said Mother directing her to the back entrance.

Racing to the old fly wire door, Rhonda flung it open. Almost instantly a furry energetic bundle came bounding up at full speed.

"Happy Birthday,' Mother called out.

Rhonda was exceptionally happy at seeing the puppy. 'This was better than a toy.' She shrieked excitedly. 'I can't believe this puppy is mine. I love him, Mum. Can he sleep with me and Robyn in our bed tonight?'

'We'll see,' Mother said.

Robyn and Rhonda often slept together. I was happy to sleep alone if it was possible. Especially when you end up with chewing gum stuck under your arm. Ouch.

Edna, who lived next door, had given us gum to chew when we'd been over for a visit after school last Thursday. We'd chewed it for over two hours, and it had long lost its taste, but we didn't care. We never got gum, so we wanted to make it last. Mother was getting annoyed and asked us to throw in the open fire in the lounge before tea. But Robyn had chewed on paper bits and had spat them in there instead. Hiding her chewy for later.

She took it to bed and lost it. Not wanting to be chastised for putting gum on the sheets, she had tricked Rhonda into swapping ends. And poor Rhonda had woken with chewy stuck under her arm and in trouble for not spitting it out. I was glad after that, to have a bed to myself. And besides I hadn't had a wet one for ages. Not so for those two.

We were ecstatic to finally have another pet in the family. Mother had not been interested in getting a pet since the tragedy of Sandy. Antoinette had killed her dog. It was too awful to talk to us about. All she would say was, "I will never forgive her." It was only years later that I found out the truth.

Antoinette had been angry at the dog for killing her chooks. Sandy was staying out on her farm. She'd taken an axe to the dog, bundled her into a sack and threw it into the river. But our Labrador had survived and had trekked five miles home looking for us, only to die from her injuries on the doorstep. How was that for a truly unbelievable act of pure evil? And certainly another contribution to my mother's mental health issues.

Mother scooped the moving fluff ball off the kitchen floor and handed him to Rhonda, who was smitten and kissed his little head. He responded with excited puppy slurps that made her giggle.

I headed out the back with Rhonda and she topped up his little tin of water that was sitting under the tap.

'You'll have to think of a name for him,' I told her.

'Yeh, maybe Fluffy? Or Snowy,' she said.

'How about you think about it,' suggested Mum. 'I'm going in make a cake for tea. Stay out and play with the pup.'

Robyn joined us and we played for ages, trying to get him to fetch objects, which he wasn't good at. So, we played tug of war with a pair of old socks we'd found in the laundry. Hopefully they weren't the Yugoslav's, or we'd probably hear about it.

Rhonda made up a little bed in the laundry from a cardboard box and some old rags that mother had out for him. And we found some old newspapers bundled in the corner to line the floor.

Standing back, it looked like a black and white alphabet carpet. Letters in small type under headings in big black font, intended to grab your attention. Printed illustrations of the latest fashions, motor cars and medicines. 'That will do, I said. Let's go inside.'

The puppy, worn out, was happy to rest in his new bed, while we enjoyed a birthday dinner. There would be no cuddles inside with him tonight.

The next morning, we raced out and opened the door of the old laundry. What a mess! The printed letters smudged. And the type torn and hard to read. Whole areas of yellow not white. Smelling of urine. "Ewww, that's disgusting. You two can clean that!" Robyn said as she stuck her head in to see what we were up to. 'I'm not touching any dog shit.'

Oh yes, Robyn could swear. I remember Robyn having her mouth washed out with soap on more than one occasion. And swearing even more while it was being implemented. I think her foul mouth came from staying out with Grandma. My grandmother was filthy, that was for sure.

Happy to see us, the puppy started running under our feet. Robyn commanded him to 'Sit!' But the puppy wasn't listening, choosing instead, to jump at our shins.

'Sit,' she said again as she pushed his bottom to show him how.

I helped Rhonda collect the soiled paper, while the pup ran around in the yard. It was time to get ready for school. We'd have to see him later.

Inside, Mother was at the sink filling the kettle. 'Sorry girls, you won't be going to school today. We're moving.'

'Again!' we all said in unison.

My heart weighed heavily in my chest already. Those two words, "We're moving" conjured up so many emotions. Loss, fear, disappointment, detachment, powerlessness, just to name a few.

My sisters and I started to complain.

'Shush! Have your breakfast and then we will pack some things.' May wasn't interested in negotiation.

We didn't want to leave again but we had no choice in adult matters.

'And we can't take the puppy. Go next door and see if the little old lady can keep him.' Since our arrival in Collingwood, we had become close to our little old spinster neighbour. She lived alone so we would pop over sometimes after school to keep her company. She would feed us lollies of the old lady type. Musk lifesavers, barley sugar and butterscotch. We enjoyed her company, and she, ours.

How could Mother give Rhonda a beautiful puppy one day, and make her give it up the next?

It was heartbreaking for Rhonda to hand over the little white puppy to the old lady next door. But she bravely did. We hadn't even named him yet.

A sweet kindly woman, we brought her close to tears as she choked on her promise to love and care for him. She handed us sweets in an attempt to make us feel better about our loss. We understood her intentions as we said goodbye and left the puppy behind.

***

THE BLUE HOUSE

May had been on the waiting list for public housing and finally there was a home available for her and the girls. She invited the Yugoslav to move in with them as well. May was sure she could hide her de facto relationship; she really didn't want to lose him. He was a good provider and a hard worker.

She was a deserted wife but migrants and working families on low wages also lived in the Commission houses. So, who would know their circumstances? They could be a migrant family with his looks. Besides she'd just hide his things if the department came for an inspection.

Her new home was a blue weatherboard house in an outer suburb of Geelong, where all the streets were names of birds. Finally, she could settle down in a comfortable home. She could afford the rent in this neighbourhood.

The added convenience of the public primary school just down the road and around the corner meant her children could walk themselves to class.

Her man had started shift work again at the Ford Factory. And after only a few weeks she had secured a job for herself at the steam laundry, starting early in the mornings.

She tried to show Robyn where the hands had to be on the clock to get her and the other two kids off to school on time. 'I have to start work early. Okay? So, you're in charge.'

But Robyn had mucked it up and had got them off to school well before the bell. May wasn't happy with her. 'I couldn't tell the time. It was your fault I got told off by the cleaner, to nick off back home.'

It looked like May would have to give them all another lesson in telling the time. She didn't want any complaints from the teachers. Her girls always learned quickly, so she was confident that they would soon get it right.

***

LEAVING HOME

I'm not sure what caused us girls to all want to leave home, but we'd talked about it and it was unanimous.

Robyn and I however were having second thoughts. We decided Rhonda should head off first. And then we would follow and catch up with her. We should have been sad, but we were happy for her.

Together we had packed up the doll's pram with things we thought we'd need for the journey. There was a supply of singlets and underpants *(We might need a change for everyday)*, a food supply of biscuits and oranges (Robyn's favourite), and lastly a bottle of raspberry cordial (*with milk added, of course*). Rhonda was ready.

'Off you go!' we ordered.

She pushed the pram to the front gate, unlatched the metal catch, and stepped out onto the pavement. 'I'm leaving now,' she shouted back.

'Yeh, see ya later. Bye!' We waved like mad to her as she continued on.

Now all we had to do was wait. We watched her as she pushed her pram towards the end of the street. At the corner, she looked both ways but didn't cross.

'What's she doing? Why won't she cross?' I said to Robyn.

'I think she's coming back,' Robyn answered.

We stood in disbelief, as we watched her turn around, and head back towards us. We didn't mind her reluctance. We were very happy to have her back as she returned through the gate. Our decision was made. We would stay for now. Running away was seriously a bit too scary.

Rhonda pushed the pram up against the side fence and forgot about it, none of us thinking to unpack its contents. We'd already moved on to our next activity.

Over the next week or so when we began complaining about the lack of underwear remaining in our cupboard, Mother sent us on a hunt around the house for them. Imagine her horror when she finally discovered them in the doll's pram outside, wet and stained with raspberry milk drink and spotted black fungus. Those lovely clean white singlets and underpants were ruined. The smell of sour milk and mould spores making her retch. She wasn't happy at all. *(Maybe now would be a time to really run away.)*

The singlets and undies could not be rejuvenated. However, we were made to wear those pink, mould-stained underclothes. And she would not buy us new ones no matter how much we complained. We were really embarrassed. There was no hanging upside down on the monkey bars with those Reg Grundies on.

***

A TIME IN HISTORY

July 21st, 1969. I was seven and a half and living in the blue house. Being a child at the time, I didn't remember it being cold, but I'm sure it was. July was the middle of winter and was generally freezing in Victoria at that time of the year.

If my sisters and I attended school on that Monday, then we had permission to walked home early. There was real excitement in households, schools, and workplaces throughout all parts of Australia. And my family were no exception.

An historic event was about to take place on planet earth.

Mother rounded us up from outside. 'Come into the lounge, girls, and sit on the floor. It's going to start.' I didn't need any extra prompting. Our school classroom had been studying this upcoming event for months now. And today it had finally arrived.

I had entered the lounge not expecting the gathering of people that were there. My eyes surveyed the small room. Half our neighbourhood were taking up space on every available chair, chattering like chimps. Not just neighbours, but work mates and friends too. Some were strangers and not known to me.

Today I shared this time in history with brief acquaintances. People who soon would be gone and forgotten. Like extras in a sci-fi movie. They were there in the background of my life, as the picture rolled.

The lights were dimmed like a movie theatre, as my sisters join me cross-legged on the floor. We didn't mind really. We were happy to have front row viewing.

The oldies began repositioning themselves in their chairs, as someone drew the curtains. A new black and white Television (*the centre of attention*) stood proud in front of us on its four wooden splayed legs. A thoroughly modern addition to our living room obtained (who knows by what means) especially for this momentous occasion.

Everyone shushed with their eyes fixated on the small screen. Weird sounds of static, and an ear-piercing whistle, made many of them squint their eyes shut.

Hadn't anyone ever told them, if you pull weird faces and the wind changes, you could be stuck looking like that forever?

Mother would tell us that all the time. Maybe I should inform them.

The screen had come to life. Not having had a television before, I was flabbergasted.

The haze kept rolling and wouldn't keep still. Fuzzy spots covered the area. Was this television ever going to show us a picture of the moon. I was beginning to think it would not.

Robyn started to jab me, always stirring up trouble if she was bored, and gaining great satisfaction from the way it annoyed me. I'm sure it was her favourite pastime.

'Stop it!' I sneered. Robyn tried to push me along the mat, so she could have the very best place on the floor. I had claimed my position early, but that didn't make any difference to her.

'Come on girls, sit still and stop fighting! There's plenty of room for everyone.' Mother tried reasoning with us.

Robyn noticed the extra adult and decided to behave herself and stop her nonsense.

The Yugoslav got up to fix the picture and we instantly shut up. He turned the antenna around in an attempt to try to pick up the best radio waves. Once he was satisfied, he placed it back on top of the set and started turning knobs on the front.

Everyone gave him a little cheer when he set it right, and a grainy picture appeared. He turned up the volume and returned to his seat on the couch. You'd swear that today he was the hero instead of those American Astronauts.

The broadcast that day was in black and white. I didn't think that was correct as I could see shades of grey as well.

No one moved a muscle, beside me, my sisters as intrigued as I. Robyn resigned herself to the fact that I wasn't budging.

Our audience's faces became transfixed like zombies, amazed at what they were seeing on our little T.V.

Neil Armstrong, Michael Collins and Edwin "Buzz" Aldrin had rocketed to the moon. The moon. It was so amazing. I couldn't believe it. The first men to land and walk its surface.

As Armstrong departed from the Lunar Module, I was glued to the screen. Would he be safe? I didn't want to witness his last gasping minutes. I held my breath at the same time trying to understand the dangers he faced.

My eyes followed his slow movements, like someone had played the movie at the wrong speed. I was thinking maybe he could have sped it up a little. We didn't have all day!

Aldrin joined Armstrong and I watched them both bouncing around on the surface of the Moon. Without Earth's gravity they were really showing off in their cumbersome spacesuits.

I thought the astronauts looked pretty awesome though, with their round basketball shaped helmets. And their pressurised white all-in-ones and massive moon boots.

They staked the American flag into the surface of the moon. Leaving their claim to history, in this outer space territory. An uncharted land they had concurred.

Michael Collins stayed in the module. His job to orbit the moon and take the photos, meant his place in this historic event was not as publicised as the other two. And I can't remember him very much either. But he was there and his contribution just as important. I watched that magic moment, as did so many around the world that day. And it secured my interest in the stars and planets ever since. I hadn't even known what an astronaut was until 1969.

I make reference to this occasion, as it was such an historical event on my timeline. And although my life was crazy and mixed up, it still had some normal moments of joy in it.

***

A HIKING TRIP

I'm not sure where mother met Dot, but Dot lived in a street that branched off from us. I liked that she had children around my age. Christopher, Gail, Merrill, and Mark attended my school, so I got to see a fair bit of them for a little while. We all became very good friends and our mothers loved visiting between the houses for cups of tea, and afternoons dabbling in the spirit world became a regular occurrence. Talk of Ouija boards, ghosts and readings kinda spooked me out, but we'd finally found friends to wander the neighbourhood with. Mother always allowed us plenty of freedom and independence.

One afternoon when Dot and her family came to visit, us children (*seven of us all up*) decided to go on a hike. We enjoyed devising activities and make-believe scenarios. None of us had ever been for a hike before. 'Why not!' I said. 'It will be fun.'

I loved an adventure and so did my sisters. We got our new friends to help pack some little cloth parcels of food. After wrapping them securely, we tied them onto sticks and slung them over our shoulder like Huckleberry Fin. We filled up a couple of bottles of cordial as well as we would certainly get thirsty. *(Everyone shared germs in those days.)*

Whilst me and the rest of the girls prepared the supplies, the boys raced home to make fishing rods— little poles with hooks on the end. 'Just in case there were fish in the city,' Mark said.

Our friends Gail and Merrill ducked inside with Robyn to tell our parents we were going hiking, while Rhonda and I waited by the gate for the boys' return.

Angela, Robyn's best friend at school arrived just as the three of them arrived back to wait with us at the gate. 'Do you wanna come?' Robyn asked.

'Sure,' Angela replied.

So, we organised her a parcel of food while we waited. And then it was time to go.

The eight of us marched off in single file, excited and looking forward to our big adventure in the city.

As we walked, we chatted merrily. Every now and again we'd sing a song and march, swinging our arms and lifting our knees up like soldiers in the army.

We covered quite a distance, our hike taking us all the way to Sparks Road and on further.

Angela started showing signs of unease.

Whatever was the matter with her? She was always a scaredy-cat, not wanting to do anything. However, Robyn was the boss and managed to get her friend to comply. Nothing new in that. Robyn always got her own way.

'Someone is following us. I can feel it,' Angela told everyone.

We all stopped and turned around, but Christopher marched forward. 'You're being a silly. Let's just keep going.' He wasn't having any of this.

But Angela wouldn't give up. 'Robyn thinks so too! Don't you, Robyn?'

Angela would have more sway if my sister agreed. Everyone one of us knew Robyn wasn't easily scared. And if she was panicked, then we'd really have something to worry about.

Mark was getting impatient. 'Come on I want to catch a fish. And it's gonna take a long time.'

We marched on and Merrill started singing. I wasn't sure if her singing was a way of pushing any paranoid thoughts to the back of her mind or what. I was spooked and joined in the singing, stopping every few minutes to look over my shoulder.

The boys were not scared and egged us on with words of encouragement and displays of their biceps.

After trekking for what seemed like ages, we came across a grassed common area. It was a pretty rugged spot. Just a mowed patch of weed-infested grass, really. The back edges near the little creek had grown long over the winter and looked like an untamed mess. It would certainly be a challenge getting down near the creek. I wasn't interested in fighting my way along that scrub to go fishing.

The boys decided we should stop here and explore. 'This looks like a place to have some fun,' said Mark. 'And I can do some fishing over there.' He pointed in the direction of the overgrown creek bed.

I was happy to rest and threw off my food swag. It was getting heavy and I was dying of thirst.

Everyone followed suit and ditched them on the grass. We shared the cordial bottles around, the boys drinking first. It was only fair because they'd carried one each to our destination, without complaint.

By the time it got to my drink, there wasn't a lot left. And as I swallowed the warm sweet liquid, it didn't really quench my dry parched throat. I was aware however that there were still two to drink, and Merrill and Rhonda were looking longingly in my direction. I resisted the temptation to scull the rest and handed it on to my sister.

A group of teen delinquents approached us as we stood finishing our dregs. We had never seen them before. Their smug faces gazed at us, holding a menacing smirk.

I tried not to stare or make eye contact as I didn't want to draw attention to myself.

With my red hair it was hard enough. I could not blend in or go anywhere without being noticed. My hair shone like a beacon or a flame of fire. Never a deterrent though, just a curiosity for lowlifes or half-wits to zone in on my innocence and vulnerability. And reining in anyone else who was in my proximity.

I don't know if I was the beacon that day, or if it was just the array of pretty little females gathered together that attracted these three male scumbags. I lowered my gaze to the ground, trying to blend into the assemblage of children.

As they approached, I was forced to lift my head, however, and acknowledge their presence.

'Hey, you kids. Yeh you, too, with the red hair. Are you listening?'

I looked skywards and dropped my eyes slowly, afraid to cast them on the ringleader.

I wasn't good at guessing ages, but fifteen to sixteen would probably be close. Certainly, old enough to carry a weapon to wave around.

I got to thinking that perhaps Angela had been right all along, and these bogans had stalked us not far from where we'd started off.

He had a cocky sure-of-himself persona. A kid that was used to walking the streets in a gang. Maybe there were more than just his two mates, and perhaps hiding somewhere nearby, ready to wreak havoc on us.

Dirty and messed up, his accomplices joined him. Their clothes could do with a wash. All had matching grease-coated hair. Whether it had been slicked back with cream or just stuck together with grime, I wasn't too sure.

The instigator was quite a bit shorter than his mates and seemed to have the biggest mouth. He boasted to us and bossed us young ones about. It was like I'd shut down his verbal taunts to protect myself from harm. His voice like a mumbled slurry of porridge churning in my ears.

His pockmarked face beamed, proud of himself as he waved his pistol about.

Meanwhile his cohorts started sneering and sniggering to exacerbate our terror. To say we were scared would not be accurate. WE WERE TERRIFIED.

None of us had ever seen a real gun before. At seven years old I couldn't fathom where they'd got them from. Maybe they'd stolen them. I assumed they were loaded with bullets, but I don't know if they were.

The other two. One tall and thin with his fashionable but filthy Levi light wash denims, pulled a revolver from the deep front pocket. His chiselled features, sour and hollow, were a good indication that he was not a friendly fellow.

The other solidly built guy had a Mo-Stache *(it would have been a moustache except it was still growing)* and thick brows over dark brown eyes. His broad flat face and slanted eyes told you this was a face from another land. He was the only one without a gun that I could see. Maybe he'd not been here long enough to steal. Or perhaps he was really good at karate chops, like the ones the boys where always practising.

Leaning in close, Christopher Mo-Stache growled his demands. 'Which of these girls is the eldest?' *(We'd all heard his words.)*

'Why'd you wanna know for?' said Chris, reeling back away from the troublemakers.

I knew it was Gail. We all did.

'Cause we want to rape her! If you let us, the rest of you go.'

These teens gave us girls the once over. Their piercing eyes and disparaging smiles were beginning to really scare me now.

I was not certain what rape was, but I knew it wasn't going to be good. Especially for Gail. They were older, taller and stronger. But most importantly they had weapons that could kill us.

I just wanted to go home.

'Run!' yelled Christopher.

The order from Christopher made me run like hell.

Maybe they'd shoot me or one of the others in the back as we ran, but I wasn't staying around to find out what they wanted. I couldn't believe how fast my short legs could run.

I was puffed and panting but covering ground rapidly. My years of outdoor activities served me well. I didn't remember them chasing us. But then I never looked back, I just kept on running.

When we got home, everyone was babbling loudly about the incident, and there was a lot of oohing and aahing. And mother went off to report it to the police.

I just wanted to sit on the couch and let them all tell the tale without me. I was too busy thanking my angels for not being shot.

***

LATCHKEY KIDS

Mother's life was getting back on track and she had been a lot happier lately. She and the Yugoslav both had jobs during the day.

We finally managed to learn the right time by the clock, so as not to arrive too early for school.

And we even managed to throw together a jam or Vegemite sandwich or something equally boring.

Well at least it didn't take up too much of my time pondering choice.

I found out later that children like us were known as latchkey kids. We were always on our own after school and before school as well. I was accustomed to it, but that's not to say that it was always trouble-free.

We would fight a lot. It was usually Robyn and me. She was good at bribing Rhonda to side with her.

She'd pull out all the stops to get her own way. Perhaps it was the fact that May had been treating her as an adult her whole life that confused her about where the line ended. Pulled up instead of brought up.

Robyn held all the responsibility. I didn't like her telling me what to do, as she always went way overboard. I guess she couldn't cope, and I didn't understand. It was always, "Go ask Robyn. Get Robyn to help you. Off you go with Robyn." There were days when Mother had slept all day. And times when the world was too hard for May to cope with. These were the days when Robyn was in charge. And I didn't understand.

Robyn enjoyed digging her nails deep into my flesh. Breaking the skin so my blood leaked from the curved shaped wounds she'd inflicted.

Kicking me was another of her favourite pastimes and she loved to lay her boots in hard if she got a chance.

But far worse than that, was her hair-pulling. She'd drag me to the floor, grabbing my hair with both her hands, tearing at my scalp and twisting strands as she pulled. I would be forced to turn onto my back and then she could drag me around. She'd show no mercy, laughing at my cries of pain. It was the best entertainment she'd had all day, and there was no stopping her now, unless I managed to escape. And then I'd lash my fury at her. But most times her cruel antics would have me beaten and nursing my wounds.

Sometimes this was the first thing May had to deal with when she arrived home. Not that she really dealt with it. She was tired from a day's work and just wanted to chill for a bit and put her feet up. The last thing mother wanted to hear were complaints about our childhood tiffs.

All of us females usually had to help with getting the dinner underway. The Yugoslav was exempt, of course, like most men of the times. He'd been working all day and it was women's work to cook the dinner.

After every mealtime, us girls did the dishes. Robyn always washed up, of course. No way she was lowering her standards to drying or putting away. That was left to Rhonda and me.

We didn't like opening the door if Mother wasn't home. We'd been taught to be wary of strangers and to ignore the knocks on the door. So we would just sit still and be quiet until they gave up and went away.

We learned how to ignite the heaters and use the electrical appliances. Mother always warned us to be careful. *She didn't want us burning the house down.*

And heaven forbid if we were sick. It could mean a lonely day at home alone. None of us girls enjoyed that, so we generally avoided telling anyone if we were.

***

GAINING TRUST

The Yugoslav was still hanging around with us. He played happy families and put on a good front. He would sit six-year-old Rhonda on his knee. Praising her for setting the table in the evening. 'You'll be my ballerina.' He cooed at her. 'The most beautiful, famous ballerina in the world.'

I didn't believe him, but Rhonda did.

He got us a white smooth-furred cat. We named her Cuddles (for obvious reasons). We loved to push her around in our doll prams. She was especially loved when we wrapped her in little woollen blankets that Robyn hand-knitted.

One day, Cuddles had little baby kittens. We raced out to see, but all we saw were little cat foetuses. All dead and clinging to their embryonic sacks.

I didn't understand what had happened to her babies. They were ugly little wet aliens lying in the dirt. She wouldn't stop with her cat meows.

I felt sorry that her babies were dead and tried to comfort her. But Cuddles couldn't be consoled and paced up and down.

It was all very sad, but the Yugoslav shushed it up and buried them against the paling fence. And Cuddles was left to deal with it.

May's boyfriend continued to groom us. Sometimes engaging and showing interest in our activities. He'd bring us home little surprises of ice-creams or sweets.

Other times he was quiet and reserved around us. He watched from a safe distance. Waiting his chance to win his prize.

He would chew and suck the inside of his cheek making a clicking sound. An annoying habit like marking time. Like a form of meditation, he stared into the distance above our head. His thought processes fantasising his next move.

Robyn didn't trust him. And I didn't either. My inbuilt radar was warning me of an unsafe environment. I didn't know what it was. No matter what, I couldn't shake the unease I felt. If mother trusted him though he must be all right.

May brought home a dog.

I'm not sure who had the naming rights of this scruffy ragged creature, but he was known as Skippy.

We adopted him from the council and saved him from his death sentence. A large breed with a shaggy black coat and sheep dog genes.

He arrived at our family and for me it was instant love. He was a special kind of dog. The type that steals your heart and distracts your mind.

Meanwhile the Yugoslav waited in the shadows of his dishonesty. His game of lies. Where he could win his prize through deception and performance.

He chose me, an obvious choice. For I was a placid, naive sort of child. Not likely to put up too much of a fight.

***

BREAKING TRUST

It was the day before Christmas and Mother had gone to do some last-minute shopping for gifts and groceries.

All the females of my house except for me had rushed out the door in a hurry to get going in the car.

Mother told me to stay behind so she and my sisters could choose an extra present for me together.

The Yugoslav was lazing about not doing anything in particular that day. Let's face it, his life was all about what time he was due at work in the factory. Maintaining the grass around our house wasn't really a job that was at the top of his priorities.

As they left the house, he relaxed in the lounge flicking through the newspaper T.V. guide, while I amused myself quietly in my room. I heard the telly switch on as he settled to watch a program.

I'd been given a new doll for my birthday only three weeks earlier. This was a child doll with mid-brown hair, a pretty blue dress, knee high socks and little white boots. Mother had added some new dolly clothes to extend her wardrobe.

Playing by myself was something I really enjoyed.

Robyn was always telling me what to do and making up the rules, but today I could play with my lovely new doll Pamela and not have to deal with her interference.

Instead of her nagging for me to engage in silly somersaults or playing mothers and fathers, I could play fashion parades and pop concerts.

I added Rhonda's entourage of dolls and busied myself lining them all up onto the bottom bunk bed. Some of them, I noticed, would need to be redressed into their finer attire. I still thought Pamela was the prettiest model of all the models. And I finished off her outfit with a colourful rainbow scarf I'd knitted myself.

My need for a drink sent me to the kitchen. I got my glass of cordial from the bottle Mother always made up in the fridge.

It was mid-afternoon and the sun was shining through the windows in the kitchen that faced north.

I wasn't watching him as he got up and crossed the room to where I was. He was muttering conversation, something about how good I was. I picked up his words as I zoned in. 'You know you special. My favourite. You always good girl. Can you keep secret? I give you surprise.'

We never had very much, so I was definitely in for a surprise. It sounded great. I could keep a secret. Didn't I always keep Robyn's secrets from Mother when she asked me? Or should I say, threatened me (she was good at intimidation). She would have been in heaps more trouble if I hadn't kept her naughty deeds to myself.

'Yep!' I said. 'I can keep a secret.'

I noticed him looking around and he was rushing out his words. 'If you want surprise, you not tell anyone, okay!' He repeated his lines just to make sure.

I agreed to keep his secret even if I didn't know what he was on about. But he got me interested in his promises of a surprise.

He grabbed my arm and directed me to get on my hands and knees on the kitchen floor. I didn't know this game and I wasn't sure why he wanted me on all fours, but I did as I was told. I didn't want him getting shitty at me and not give me a surprise.

What did he want me to do? I wasn't sure this was a good game. I was trying to fit all the pieces together in my mind. It didn't feel right somehow.

I had been warned against strange men, but this man was part of my family. I had no idea that trust could be broken by people I knew. And at eight years old I knew nothing about the sexual intentions of males.

'This maybe hurt a bit. You keep still,' he said.

Hurt! What was he going to do that would hurt me? He hadn't mentioned hurt before!

I was trying to work it out and suddenly I wanted to get up onto my feet. But I couldn't move, as he had me firmly in his grasp. I started to shake. What the hell was happening?

He didn't take off my underpants but moved them aside instead. He held me firmly from behind. The Yugoslav was trying to push something inside my body, and I could feel my bottom stinging. I started complaining, wriggling, trying to get away. Then sounds of whimpering escaped me as my tears flowed, running down my face. I was afraid, confused. What was he doing? I wanted to scream but I didn't. I tried to pull away again. And then he suddenly stopped.

He bellowed at me to get up off the floor. *Thank goodness that was over.* I tried to stand properly and take my focus off the smarting that I felt in my rear.

Why was he upset with me? I'm the one *he* hurt. Would I get my surprise? Somehow, I knew I wouldn't.

My family tramped through the door in a noisy scurry of excitement and mayhem. But I was silent and stunned like a tranced invisible spirit. It was like I had left my body and everyone around me were extras, babbling things that didn't make any sense.

I couldn't see him. It was like I'd snuffed him out of the picture as I stood there alone.

My mother raced over and wrapped her arms around me.
'What's happened?' she said darting her head around to check
his reaction.

I still couldn't see him, and my head spun and my heart beat
fast. I tried to breathe but it felt like the air had been sucked out
of my body.

'Bend over!' Mother shrieked as she bent me over. I nearly
collapsed in her grasp with relief. She started cursing which
upset me more. What had I done to make her so upset?

Perhaps the Yugoslav had run off while Mother was
attending to me as I didn't see him at all. I just remember being
rushed out the door and into the car with my sisters close
behind. To say May was frantic was an understatement. She
drove like a woman obsessed, straight to the doctor's clinic. It
was a miracle it was still open, seeing it was so close to
Christmas.

I was full of confusion and my sisters were asking, 'What's
up!'

What had I done that had made my mother so angry?

The Yugoslav had done something bad to me, but I still
wasn't sure what it was. I hadn't seen what he was doing.

The doctor was asking questions, and I could tell it was
serious. My bottom was sore, and the doctor wanted to look at
it.

After my examination, the doctor took my sisters in, to
checked them out as well. After which the police arrived to talk
to all of us.

I was taken aside with Mother for questioning. And even
though the officers were nice to me, it was frightening and
embarrassing talking about my private bits.

It felt like a nightmare. Why was I in big trouble and having
to answer all their questions? And what if the Yugoslav was
angry at me for telling his secret. I was so upset, I just wanted
to cry.

At nine years old, Robyn was not happy being examined in such a private area. She demanded an explanation. And Mother told her that the doctor was checking for worms. But Robyn could sniff out a coverup real well and continued to harp May until Mother became cross, and silenced her, refusing to elaborate any further on the issue.

The doctor, and then the police, wanted to get into an in-depth conversation. All of them firing questions at me while they took notes.

I was actually frightened, scared as hell that I had committed some terrible act. I spent what seemed like an eternity listening to grownups, and going back over the event. Trying to find the words to explain what he did.

After my interrogation it was all hushed up and not spoken of again until the court case sometime later.

I am sure it was an attempt to cause me minimal trauma at the time, but it only made me feel shame at upsetting everybody. It took me a lifetime to absorb the true crime of that day and begin to understand the impact it had on my life.

But I had no control as an eight-year-old. The Yugoslav had been interrupted. I've got to be thankful for that.

***

A STRESSFUL NIGHT

What a horrendous day for my family that Christmas Eve. A time of joy turned into a time of dolefulness and an agony of mind. No one could predict the situation that my mother's lover put us all in. Where would we go right on Christmas when everything closed for the festive season.

Reeling up feelings that my mother had buried deep inside her conscience and bringing up the dread in her heart. May was very upset.

She took us to Melbourne that night and we all stayed at Aunt Virginia's. I curled up on the back seat, falling asleep from sheer exhaustion on the drive down. I was sick of answering their never-ending questions about him. I didn't know what they wanted. If only I could fill my ears with cotton wool and just nod yes even though no sound could penetrate. Maybe that would make them stop hassling me.

Someone carried me in whilst I slept, but I awoke a couple of hours later.

My stomach was sore as I flung my tired limbs from the bed and tried to stand. The pain shot through me from my rib cage to my back passage. Doubling over, I wandered the hall stooped over like a hunchback in the fairy-tale. Instead of a fish bone stuck in my windpipe I had a dagger in my intestines.

The pain continued to shoot through me as I searched for my mother. Navigating my way by sound, listening for a voice I could recognise, I gravitated to the thin strip of light that shone on the carpet under the wooden door. I was nearly there when I heard my mother speaking. It drew me closer to my destination. It was dark in the hall and I wasn't really familiar with the layout of the house, since my only visits to Aunt Virginia had been during the day.

I opened the door as it gave out a moanful squeak. Its old hinges had dropped a little over its forty-something years of use.

The adults grew silent as I entered with eyes filled with tears.

I immediately felt the warmth of the open fire. December was shaping up to be a little cool this year.

The couch faced the fire so as to capture as much heat as possible for anyone who rested there. Its bright orange and yellow flames danced in the hearth, I was mesmerised, and its warmth instantly calmed me enough to blurt out my words without sobbing. 'My tummy is sore.'

Not waiting for an invite, I climbed up onto the couch to snuggle next to Mum. 'It really hurts.'

She placed her hand on my forehead like she always did when she wanted to gauge if I was as sick as I made out. Generally she made up her mind if I was putting it on or not by feel.

'Nope, no temperature.' She assured me in her matter-of-fact voice.

I had relaxed but now that dagger was twisting its blade inside my bowel, I screeched in agony.

'Best take her into the hospital,' Virginia said as she got up to grab her keys. 'Come on, I'll take you. Gordon will be here to hold the fort.'

I was bundled into the car with a blanket to keep me warm. The night was cool after leaving the confines of the house. So I snuggled in the rug and remained silent for the rest of my journey, arriving a short time later.

After examination, I was issued with medication to clear my bowel. The Yugoslav had created a painful few days for me. Distress and anxiety plagued me much longer than just one or two days.

***

A CRIMINAL GOES TO JAIL

Our Christmas Day was belated that year. Santa never came near us in Thornbury. After all, I hadn't been good enough. I figured it was my fault we weren't sitting under our green pine tree that the Yugoslav had purchased and opening our Christmas presents.

Did Santa even come to babies? Because I never saw any presents for my baby cousins, Lucy and Cathy.

But maybe Aunt Virginia had hidden them until we all left for home again. After all, baby Lucy didn't know which day was Christmas and Cathy still wasn't three till March. It would be easy to fool the both of them and save us the distress.

I'd fallen asleep on the return journey home from hospital the night before.

And after being given pain relief, I hadn't heard anything. Santa's reindeer could have been dancing a jig and I wouldn't have been any the wiser.

I loved visiting Aunt Virginia she was always kind to me. And I enjoyed nursing little Lucy and tickling her tummy. Or making farting noises on her arms with my lips. Lucy would squirm and tell me, 'More,' as we'd giggled together.

Aunt Virginia's swivel chairs in the kitchen were always too tempting. They were a luxury item we never had.

Along with my sisters, I enjoyed the dizzy feeling they gave us as we spun them around, often falling off onto the floor like a drunken man after a session at the local.

She would chastise us in a grumpy voice, but we knew she was more bark than bite.

Mother got a phone call from the Yugoslav. Or maybe it was the police. Anyhow she knew where to find him in Coburg. And we drove to see him.

Now you would think that she would never want to see him again. Usually if someone assaults your daughter that's a pretty good indication that they were not to be ever trusted again.

And you certainly wouldn't want to put your daughter through any more trauma.

But she took us to the jail. A massive bluestone building with a tower each side of a roller door and walls that reached the sky. A big sign sat between them that said *HM PRISON PENTRIDGE.*

We entered through the administration door that sat to the side. Mother went through the usual jargon required to enter a prison. Like a security pat down and some identification. She must have deceived them using our birth name and not Bruce like she'd brainwashed us to be.

I'm sure I wasn't supposed to be visiting the Yugoslav while he was on remand.

We were directed into a room full of echoes. Or maybe it was my thoughts screaming inside my head I heard. Just one chair to share between four, as we waited for that criminal to appear.

I was fidgety and nervous. I figured I had put him here in this jail, and he'd be so mad at me when he saw me. I hated confrontation and I was sure he would have angry words with me. I shivered at the thought.

We all stood there surprisingly quiet, like we might get locked up too, if we didn't shut our mouths.

Suddenly he appeared behind the glass booth we had been facing. I didn't know from where he came, just that he was there.

Mother dragged me onto her knee so I could talk to him.

He was trying to get my attention, but I held my head down not wanting to look at him. I was trying to pretend I was listening when in fact I wanted to run, to hide from him I didn't want to be there or listen to him anymore.

I slid off my mother's knee, moving Rhonda to the front for her turn, and stood behind the huddle to block his view. I stood there trying to erase that horrid event of that day from my memory.

And when it was time to go and he waved us good-bye, I hoped that would be the end of it. But it wasn't.

***

A COURT HEARING

The court hearing was scheduled just a few short months after the event. March. Cathy would be three this month. I knew her birthday.

I tried to think of Cathy having her cake. It made me happy and helped me forget about all these strange people talking to me about things I'd buried and wanted to forget.

I'd forgotten what happened last Christmas Eve. Hadn't Mother told me to. She didn't want me telling anyone about what he'd done. And I did what I was told.

'All you have to say is that you can't remember,' Mother told me repeatedly.

If I believed it, it could disappear from my mind forever. "POOF" it would vanish like magic.

May wanted him out of prison. Somehow, he had convinced her to side with him. I'm not sure what power he had over her. Was she scared of being alone with her mind, her demons from the past. The struggles with money and homelessness.

If we could convince the jury of his innocence, then she would work it all out once he was released.

She'd put one man in jail, maybe she couldn't put another. I don't know why she made me lie. But I did.

They knew they had him. Why else would they put me on the stand. I was their hope of conviction. And I lied, though I didn't want to. And when I placed my hand on the Bible in the witness box, my whole self was angry at me for swearing to tell the truth, the whole truth and nothing but the truth. And then I lied.

They asked me, and every question, I answered, "I don't remember".

So, he was acquitted on all charges and released.

**

A CAR

The station wagon was quite a recent purchase.

'I got a car loan,' my mother told me. Trouble was she never did pay any repayments on it.

Well maybe one or two, but I wasn't really sure about that either. In fact, it could have been stolen. With so many untruths being told, it was quite possible.

The Yugoslav had just been released from his imprisonment, and now he was here in our blue house. I hadn't been told that he was coming back, but he had shown up this morning. Like he'd never been away. Coming inside and making himself at home in the kitchen.

I disappeared pretty quickly outside to play, preferring to ignore him. He and my mother seemed to disregard the fact that I was still very traumatised from his assault on me, around twelve weeks previously.

I didn't want him here with us. And now she was making me stand next to him, to get my picture taken. When I'd really rather just go off and continue with my activities.

'Linda, move closer so I can get you all in the picture. I want to take a good shot of the wagon behind you all,' Mother said as she nudged me along. 'Look up. Rhonda, you too.'

It was hard to get a perfect snap that day. As the rays were bright, and I was looking directly into the sun.

I tilted my head down and away from him, feeling uncomfortable at having my body close to his. But I held my eyes upwards to satisfy Mother's requests, and this seemed to do the trick.

Click! It was done.

'Now for one of me in a photograph.'

Thank goodness!

***

THE BUS TRIP

My sisters and I were very excited. Our holidays, up until now, had always been to Deniliquin visiting family.

Mother was compelled to travel home regularly so we could spend time with our father. Our father Cyril had never bothered to obtain a motorcar licence. So, it was left to May to organise the reunions and be the responsible parent.

We were not financial enough to holiday anywhere else anyhow. No one I ever knew took holidays anywhere. So when Mother explained that we would be travelling to the western parts of Australia, I was ecstatic.

It could have been anywhere, and I'd have thought it exotic. But to be promised a trip through this region of Australia, conjured up thoughts of Aboriginal men throwing spears and boomerangs, and deserts of orange sand dunes like the Sahara Desert— void of everything.

I had learnt about our landscapes and Aboriginal people at school, but I soon found out my understanding of indigenous people was not really accurate, and that the Australian desert in fact was full of native shrubs and teaming with wildlife. Definitely nothing like the African one that I had envisaged.

We all loved a road trip. I was used to spending hours in the car. We'd be singing at the tops of our voices, or fighting and arguing. Nothing in between.

Sometimes mother would threaten to pull over and leave us on the side of the road. Of course, she did follow through with her threat a couple of times, but she would always turn the car around, to pick us up again.

Did my sisters and I learn the lesson? Not really. We knew she was only bluffing and would never really leave us.

Today we would be travelling on a greyhound coach. Full of elation, I scampered onto the bus. Mother headed towards the back to find some seats.

Rhonda sat at the very back with Mother while I moved into the seat directly in front of them. And as I watched through a side window, I noticed another passenger snaking up a line on the other side of the bus.

I stared out at another empty bus parked beside us inside the dingy depot. Robyn was beside me blocking any view of the aisle. But I heard people climb the steep metal steps.

Some travellers were still getting settled and I was a little restless. I was anxious to start our ride as the interior space was getting noisier by the minute.

Hopefully, once the wheels started turning, and the bus drove out through the city, everyone would settle. Perhaps the sights of Melbourne would create distraction and entertainment for everyone.

Robyn started bossing me for the window seat. She held a higher position in the family and, as usual, thought it her birthright.

I started complaining to Mother. 'Robyn is being mean. She is scratching and digging her nails into me.'

Robyn snarled and screwed up her face. And she cursed me in a loud whisper. 'Just move out of the way, fatty.' She loved to throw insults to get her way. 'I'm sitting near the window. And if you don't move, I'll pull your hair.'

My sibling loved to grab handfuls of my hair to assert her authority. I knew it was coming so I ducked forward out of the way as she attempted a demonstration.

'Robyn you stop that right now!' came the voice of my mother. 'Let Linda have a turn first by the window and then you can swap around later on.' This suggestion was not taken up and Robyn continued her torturous antics.

She loved to see how long it took before I would give up and allow her to have her own way. But today I was standing my ground and refusing to be intimidated.

After another stern warning for trying to drag me off the seat, Robyn gave in. Deciding a move beside Rhonda might be a victorious pursuit. Asking Mother if she could swap and sit with Rhonda freed me up from her bullying.

There was minimal resistance from Rhonda and so Mother was satisfied. At least now she could save herself the embarrassment of her children arguing and fighting in public.

Growing up, Robyn and Rhonda held a special bond, from which I was excluded. They would play games and choose each other over me. I could never win an argument, as they would gang up together.

People even said they looked alike, whereas I looked different. I always felt like the odd wheel.

The door closed and the driver began nesting his backside into his seat, ready for the long drive. It would be hours before he'd be able to get up and have a rest again.

He announced his name and welcome everyone aboard. Then he gave a running commentary on the scheduled stops and the expected arrival time at each destination. He started the engine, the bus rattled into life and we were on our way.

I always loved the start of a long commute. It was always the best. The anticipation of what would happen and what you would see along the way always created excitement.

But very soon into my bus trip, it became apparent that I was stuck in this time capsule. Unable to get out until I'd done my time. The brief stops only allowed mere minutes to stretch my body, or to use the bathroom.

We were going the long haul, so Mother had packed us a variety of snacks and drinks. Our sandwiches were simple— honey, peanut butter, jam or Vegemite, with margarine and day old bread. Mother wrapped the sandwiches in waxed paper that really didn't help the freshness. I hated margarine, preferring to just pick holes in my bread and eat it plain. The spreads would all run into the oily margarine by the time you ever got to eat it. And the honey was stiff and grainy like sweet beach sand jammed between cardboard. They were the pits. (Sandwiches have certainly come a long way.)

May was not a coffee drinker, so it was always tea. She would make a sweet and milky tea, brewed in a thermos flask for all to share.

Whenever we stopped near a water tank, we could get a drink of water straight from the tap— no cup needed.

Everyone smoked inside the buses in those days, so cigarette smokers puffed away happily for the duration of the journey.

Meanwhile I was compelled to passive smoke whether I liked it or not. The smell of burning tobacco ingrained in my hair and clothing and lingered for hours after I left the bus.

During that day, I slept on and off. May dosing me with travel sickness medication, meant I found it hard to stay awake at times.

The last few months had been exhausting and unsettling, but today I could finally relax.

I slept for hours as the afternoon dragged on and the coach travelled across the state.

The driver released travellers from their impoundment at various locations and added others to serve their time.

It was a monotonous day sightseeing out of the dusty windows or catching glimpses of people from across the aisles. The only noise, knitting needles clicking in my ears, or the howling of a naughty child that wouldn't behave.

Hours later I slept soundly to the rhythm of the bus, and Mother startled me as she suddenly spoke. 'Look who it is,' she said with excitement in her voice.

Leaning over the seat to the back, she attempted to get my sisters' attention as well. Pointing out the window and beckoning them to look.

Surely not, I couldn't believe it! The Yugoslav was following us in our new Ford Station Wagon.

I turned around and propped myself on my knees.

There was Skippy, our black sheep dog, with his head extended out of the back seat window and the Yugoslav waving madly. His arm extended and held high out of the driver's side window, as he drove alongside the coach, it seemed signalling aggressively for the driver to stop.

But the driver would not pull up his bus *(much to the annoyance of the Yugoslav)*. And the Yugoslav sped off, an obvious look of aggression flashing on his face on his way past.

It was dark as the bus wound its way through the Adelaide Hills. The twinkling lights in the valley spread out like distant stars in the galaxy. I was impressed by the beauty of this capital city in South Australia. And the adventure of it all.

***

A CARAVAN

We slept by the roadside that night and the next day made our way to Ceduna on the fringe of the Nullarbor, arriving at our destination in the late afternoon, and the Yugoslav met us. Mother was keen to shop to get something to eat for dinner. We didn't explore anything at all as they were anxious to check in at a local Caravan Park for some rest.

The Yugoslav had been whispering to May as we travelled along. I hadn't heard any of it, but I just knew something was brewing.

'Wait with your girls. I organised somewhere to sleep,' the Yugoslav said. We sat and waited, too tired to utter a word.

'They have one van in the back. We drive over. Come, I show you, May!' he said. Returning to the front seat, he began ordering us, without even looking around. 'You girls hide!'

'Yes, put your heads down!' said Mother taking over the conversation. 'They mustn't see you.'

We ducked, bowing our heads below window level.

I was surrounded by large glass frames, making hiding from view very difficult. Luckily darkness started to fall, or I'm sure we'd have been seen.

He drove in along the track toward the sea and pulled up in front of a shiny white caravan.

Leaving the car, the Yugoslav climbed the little metal steps of the van and opened the door, with Mother right behind him, anxious to get a look inside.

'You three stay there. I'm going to look for the toilet. When I find it, I'll come and get you,' Mother called out.

I waited with my sisters for her return. Meanwhile the Yugoslav busied himself emptying the contents of the car.

'I'm busting,' I said to Robyn.

'Me too,' said Rhonda. 'Bad luck. You have to wait.'

We both began jiggling around and crossing our legs together. I became desperate, trying really hard not to wet my pants right there on the seat.

I tried to focus on anything but urinating, but urgency is distracting. Squeezing my muscles tight, I prayed for Mother's return, relieved when finally, she arrived.

She pointed. 'Over there.'

I was off. Racing to the amenities.

Inside the van we were treated to a feed, and soon it was time for bed. 'Go to bed girls,' the Yugoslav said, staring with those mad eyes.

I was happy to go. Not because he told me to, but because I was spent. I did not want to conform to his commands. I would tell my mother if he dared threaten me. That was for sure.

'Wake up. It's time,' he whispered. He shook Mother awake. 'Give me help to hook it. We can't fool round,' he said in his broken English.

I had been asleep in my bed. Robyn and Rhonda had bunked together as usual, and had not been roused by the disturbance. They still lay sleeping peacefully adjacent to me. I tried to listen to the conversation, but fatigue soon overwhelmed me, and I drifted into slumber again.

***

THE THEFT

May was instantly awake and ready to go. Maybe she hadn't really been asleep.

May snuck quietly from the van. Through the darkness outside, she could hear the sound of the ocean as it lapped gently against the shoreline. The moon lit the sky a little, enough for her to see the silhouette of her man and the faint white of the car panels.

'Hop in car,' he whispered. Opening the front driver side, she felt the adrenaline building. *Shit, we'd better not get caught.* She closed the door and turned on the ignition.

Moving the column shift to reverse, she carefully backed the station wagon up against the caravan and he hitched it on with skill and precision.

It went miraculously well. She sighed with relief when he jumped in behind the wheel. Not wasting anytime, she slid over quickly to let him in.

As he towed them out of the park, the children still tucked up inside, she marvelled at his genius.

As they drove, however, her mind started to race a thousand kilometres an hour. What if the other campers heard them? Her hand flew to her racing heart. Would the caravan park owners run out and stop them? Her head spun. But then she figured they wouldn't question it until the morning, when they would awake to see a space left by the caravan's absence. People were always coming and going in a tourist park. May started to calm down.

A brilliant plan and he executed it perfectly. They travelled all night with the girls still tucked up in their beds. And they would be way out of sight before anyone could work out what had happened.

***

THE NULLARBOR

From Ceduna we travelled across the Nullarbor. I jumped out when we stopped at the roadhouse. It was early in the morning and I needed a toilet and something to eat. The Yugoslav needed to fill up the wagon while I went to pee.

I then entered the roadhouse to find my mother. She gave me a few cents to buy sweets and assured me we'd eat a little further along the way.

As I followed her around, she instructed me to grab a bottle of cordial and a packet of sweet biscuits. She purchased some canned beans, spaghetti and Spam. She also picked up a packet of tea and a tin of Sunshine Powdered Milk. I knew if I got the chance to get near that tin of milk, I'd certainly polish it off by the spoonful.

The Yugoslav placed a couple of jerrycans full of fuel in the corner of the back space. And he spoke to Mother. 'We have bulk water and petrol.'

The Nullarbor Plains covered over 770 square miles (2000 square kilometres), the man at the register had told the Yugoslav as he paid for the supplies. 'I suggest you be prepared. You will need to refuel somewhere during your crossing. And take plenty of water. It's essential across that wilderness. Roadhouses are far and few between, and you might not see a car for days if you break down.'

The Yugoslav ordered us into the van. I whined about it. I wanted to travel in the car, but mother backed him and, reluctantly, I entered the metal prison along with my sisters.

Skippy had had time to explore the area before jumping in to join us. Plonking himself over on one of the beds. *Nothing but comfort for Skip.*

We headed off again down the road— not much more than a dusty corrugated track with a landscape denuded of trees. A straight stretch of semi-arid desert dotted with saltbush and native vegetation. Not that I got to see very much of it travelling in a caravan.

I stuck my nose against the glass pane of the tiny window above my bed and watched as long as I could, but I was getting jerked about and my face kept getting smashed up against the surface as the van careened over the potholes.

The temperature rose and I became drowsy as we headed westbound. The travel sickness tablets were starting to take effect. Robyn and Rhonda were already dozing on the other single bed and I lay down too. Skippy moved sprawled out on the Lino, in an attempt to cool his furry body.

I woke to the sound of thumping wheels on the road. I could tell we were still travelling in a straight line without any turns.

The heat in the van seemed extreme, and orange dust covered its interior. Like a fine talc powder, it was everywhere. Footprints in the orange marked my path as I walked to the sink to pump a drink from the tap. The little bench top where I'd placed my hand to steady myself, had my print etched in the dust like a work of stencilled art. And the bench seat and table were also smothered.

Returning to the little glass window, I found it smudged with orange earth and impossible to view through. The suffocating air made me cough and gasp. I needed to get some relief. Suddenly I just wanted to get out of this choking tin can on wheels.

How could I let my mother know that we all needed to get out? We couldn't open the window and wave something to flag her down, as the dust was just too thick and visibility impossible.

Opening the window would only increase the amount of dust inside our prison.

My siblings and I were trapped. Imprisoned at the mercy of our captors.

I was not the only one suffering. My sisters, too, were feeling hot and dusty, coughing and spluttering as the dust entered their airways.

Our nose secretions ran red like blood. Wiping them on a towel that was lying about, we left red tinged snot trails in the weave.

It was all getting very uncomfortable. Poor Skippy wasn't really coping as he sat whining to get out, over by the door. His water bowl slid around on the floor, constantly tipping over and adding to the mess.

Perhaps the Yugoslav was hoping he'd be rid of us once and for all. Kill us from dehydration in the back of the caravan. And then he could just bury us out there on the plains. He might even get away with it.

I didn't trust him and couldn't understand why we were still in his company. Hadn't he gone to prison for hurting me? I was still contemplating what to do when suddenly the car pulled over and the van came to an unexpected stop.

Mother threw open the door as the dog and the three of us leaped out in one heap.

Spluttering up red stained mucus and gasping in the cooler air, I jumped from one foot to the other, trying to hold in the pee.

Mother's eyes grew wide and her jaw dropped. "Oh shit. I didn't realise the dust was so bad. Girls, are you okay?"

'I wanna pee!' was all I could call out.

'Behind the caravan.' Mother pointed.

I didn't need to waste any more time. I headed to the back of the van and sat squatting alongside my sisters. As I urinated, I stared at the exterior walls of the portable home. It was totally covered in soil from top to bottom. No longer white but a dull dusty orange, with a matching station wagon to pull it.

The afternoon was fading, and the night would soon approach. I sat around and sipped on water and ate baked beans for tea before I climbed back aboard the tin-mobile and slept amongst the dust.

In the morning, Mother gave the bedding a thorough shake out, and the floor got a clean with a bit of rag. My sisters and I helped by wiping down the surfaces. Robyn washed up the dishes.

As for all of us, we'd have to wait for a water hole or a roadhouse tank before we'd be able to be clean ourselves again.

After a breakfast of rice bubbles and powdered milk, we were on our way again. I still stayed in the caravan along with the others. Mother had shown us how to stuff a towel against the door where most of the dust had blown in underneath.

It didn't completely eradicate the problem but certainly helped. And Mother's insistence for the Yugoslav to stop more frequently, allowed us short periods out of confinement to toilet or stretch our legs. He even permitted us short stints of travel in the wagon that day.

His paranoia of getting caught was the reason for our misery. No-one was following our stolen caravan, so he needn't have worried. The Nullarbor had very little traffic. During our journey, we were almost completely alone.

And there wasn't much hope in anyone recognising the vehicles. Not with the layers of dirt that covered them.

In the late afternoon we pulled off onto the shoulder of the road to rest and eat. Mother emptied the heated canned food into bowls from the van, and we shared oranges and sweet biscuits.

The Yugoslav had devised an ingenious way to heat the cans' contents by placing them on top of the engine while he was driving, and he could time it so they would be piping hot and ready to eat when we were.

With the nights on the Nullarbor cooling considerably, we would all sit on the ground and watch the magnificent sunsets that painted the Australian sky. A lovely time to just enjoy the drop in temperature and the stillness at the end of a gruelling day.

My ears would hiss of nothingness. I searched for sound. Yes maybe, just maybe I could faintly hear the dingoes call.

A vast open space. A land that someone had forgotten to furnish.

I loved the Nullarbor with its total isolation, its harsh flat landscape, and all its dust. A massive plain of limestone, where only tough salt and blue bush grew, and rainfall was scarce.

Unique animals roamed its earth. I looked for them, but all I saw on that stretch of road was the odd emu in the distance and the red kangaroo.

At night, the blackened sky delightfully shone a billion stars down on me. A vivid contrast from my daytime hours of red dust and blue skies.

There were caves and sink holes too, but I never got to see them either.

It took us four days or maybe it was five. Who knows when you're young? The Yugoslav was in a hurry, but the rough road wouldn't allow us to speed. Night driving was far too dangerous. With bounding kangaroos, stray wildlife and very few people travelling on the road, you could do some serious damage to yourself and your vehicles. Speed was avoided altogether.

One day, we were forced to all pile out onto the road while the Yugoslav changed the rear flat tyre that was badly worn from the harsh terrain. It lay useless and discarded where we stood.

There were days too when the radiator overheated, and we'd be forced to stand with the bonnet up until it cooled enough for him to fill it up with water. Out on the plains, the odd windmill and a water tank or two broke the monotony, but little else appeared on the long dusty road.

I stood in the open plains like an alien, kidnapped and alone in some far-flung planet. Mars maybe? Wasn't the Mars surface red with nothing there but more of the same? Kinda like here.

***

DON'T TALK TO ANYONE

The Yugoslav drove us all to the border. South Australia on our side and Western Australia on the other.

'I'm not throwing my oranges in the fruit bins,' Robyn whispered to me, after Mother had instructed her to get rid of them at the agriculture checkpoint.

'I've eaten them all,' she replied. Truth was in fact, that she had hidden them under her clothing, and smiled with glee at her fib a little way down the highway. Robyn loved oranges and she wasn't going to throw them out for anyone.

Mum took a turn at driving as we proceeded west. Another arduous day running into the other, with fights and arguments commonplace now inside the van, from boredom and confinement.

Robyn had starting her reign of terror towards me. She used her lion-like claws to puncture my wrists as she tried to hold me down on the bed. With her knee, she clamped my torso to the mattress.

I began kicking my legs madly, but I was unable to make contact as she pinned me firm. I rolled with her as hard I could, and we landed with a bump on the van floor. Her body slamming hard as the van hit a bump in the road.

Now she was mad.

I ran. But there was nowhere to hide.

She caught me and grabbed a handful of hair, as I attempted to scream the caravan walls in.

She didn't care if she hurt me and would spit angry foul words in my ears, all the while enjoying the spectacle she created.

She won, and I surrendered, allowing her to finish her onslaught.

I dropped to the floor as she gripped my hair and bent me backwards with her foot on my spine. It hurt, but I would not cry. I sulked instead and dobbed her in when I got the chance.

As night fell, we rested near the town of Norseman, amongst the gums that surround the town. The Yugoslav built a little fire out of gum sticks and we huddled around it. Not so much for warmth but because it was comforting.

And Mother made tea for everyone, sweetened with sugar and lightened with powdered milk.

And somehow it made the day worth it.

They woke at six and hustled us out. 'Today,' the Yugoslav said, 'we go to Perth.'

But the car was making noises like it was going to shake apart and the Yugoslav told Mother, 'We go inland to closest town. Hope we get mechanic to look at it. Perth too far.'

He crawled along at a snail's pace towards the mining town of Kalgoorlie. Every bump threatened to do more damage.

I enjoyed being in the wagon, and wound the windows right down to feel the warm wind blow through my tangled hair. I had told mother about the fighting last night before bed and she had thought it best we all travelled with them today.

Today we all sang for joy, enjoying our freedom. Yesterday's problems done and forgotten.

The Yugoslav hid the caravan off the road and just on the outskirts. It was easily camouflaged with its red covering of earth and blended in nicely with the surrounding landscape.

'We come back later today,' he assured us.

The station wagon barely made it into the town. It really needed a mechanic to look it over. The rutted roads had really played havoc with its front end, and it would have to be left for repair for at least a day or possibly more.

He dropped us off at a little supermarket to buy supplies and he went to find a mechanic and talk to the locals. 'Not a long time. We go back to the caravan soon,' he said.

Yugoslav took the dog and returned later with a pair of shearing scissors so he could give Skippy's coat a trim.

Kalgoorlie's main street was flat, wide and straight. From where I stood, I could view the whole street, one end to the other. I'd never seen anything like this outback town before.

Its buildings were extremely old, but they had once been grand. And Mother told me they had been built when the town was rich with gold.

It felt like a dream, after days travelling on the plains. I wanted to explore it more and maybe find my own gold.

But mother warned me. 'Linda and Rhonda, you stay here and wait for the Yugoslav. Don't talk to anyone! Especially the police.'

I didn't want to wait for him. But what else could I do? Robyn had run ahead and yelled, 'In here.'

And when Mother had nodded "yes" she had disappeared inside.

'How come Robyn gets to go inside?' I asked Mother.

She just shrugged and disappeared too.

Rhonda and I were chatterboxes, it was hard not to talk to people who wanted to talk to you.

Robyn on the other hand was much more stand offish and could avoid talking to us for days. She'd have no trouble ignoring anyone.

The instruction caused me to feel hot and cold and then my chest tightened. How long would I have to stand out here and wait for the Yugoslav, while they shopped? He might kill Skippy dog, and then come back and drag us both into the scrub. It would be easy to make his escape and just take off. We didn't know where he had taken the wagon. He could have hidden it where he was going to kill us, for all I knew. I felt paranoid and the heat was making me feel faint. I swallowed hard and tried to erase the feelings of dread that were creeping in.

I hung onto the old hardwood post that formed part of the roof structure of the veranda, trying to calm myself. An Aboriginal man came up to talk to Rhonda. Her pretty blonde hair and round cheeky face perhaps drawing his attention. It was true that Deniliquin had an indigenous population. But we were very small when we were living there. And on holidays we never took any notice. We were too busy out on the farm playing.

I don't think it was just that his face was dark that terrified Rhonda. It was the fact that she'd been warned not to talk to everyone. And this stranger was getting friendly. She was only six and ran into the shop. I happily followed her inside. I didn't want to be out there alone waiting for the Yugoslav to kidnap me. Or to have this strange man hanging around.

'That black man out there wants to kidnap me!' Rhonda blurted out to the woman behind the counter.

'What black man?' The woman smiled in amusement.

Rhonda pointed to the man standing out on the street.

'Oh no, he wouldn't hurt you,' she replied. 'He's a nice man.' She tried to reassure Rhonda.

144

I'm not sure we believed her as we huddled inside near the door until he moved off and Mother showed up at the counter to pay just in time. The Yugoslav had arrived, and I shuddered as I watched from my place in the store. We were ready to go, and ventured out into the street again, the Aboriginal man forgotten.

We'd have to wait until tomorrow for the car. Yugoslav man assured us that he'd walk into town early and drive it back repaired. 'Get ready,' he said. 'I hook up and we go. Police be after us if we not hurry.'

So, we spent the rest of the day and night hidden as we had a nervous wait.

***

SKIPPY GETS A HAIRCUT

We were all exhausted when we arrived back at the van. Walking from town in the heat was extremely tough. And poor Skippy with his thick shaggy black coat was really distressed. Although we were travelling in the cooler months of the year and the night temperatures were quite cold, it still got hot in the middle of the day. Skip's thick bushy coat proved a real hindrance.

The Yugoslav liked animals, so he couldn't bear to see the dog huffing and sprawled out trying to cool himself under the shrubs on the parched ground. The sun was still high and what little vegetation was about, cast very little shadow.

He brought out the pair of sheep shears— like two knives joined together with metal sprung handles. I made a mental note to watch where he stowed these. I didn't want him murdering us all with the shears in the middle of the night. Holding the dog like a true shearer between his legs on the ground, he went to work on shearing Skip's fur.

'Giving Skip haircut, May!' he shouted. 'The dog dying out here. May! Come give me help.'

Us girls stood around to watch the spectacle.

He was very matted by now and hadn't had a bath in weeks. Come to think of it, I wasn't sure when our last bath had been either.

It wasn't going to be an easy task.

Coaxing Skip with soft words and kisses to his muzzle, Mother knelt in front of the dog and held his head with both hands while the Yugoslav clipped away.

Skip was happy to sit and receive attention for a little while, but soon became bored and dropped down and rolled to the side.

'Perfect. I shear you this side now. Good Skip.'

But Skippy had had enough. This was a game. Rolling over onto his back, he began kicking his legs and barking. It was all fun and games.

We tried not to laugh, but it was quite entertaining.

After an escape and chase around, we managed between us to pin him down and complete the task.

He looked like a patchwork of art, but it didn't matter. He was at least a cool masterpiece of geometrical fur.

Early the next morning, the Yugoslav retrieved the wagon from town, he threw the shears along with some cooking utensils into the back of the wagon and hitched the caravan. We were on our way again.

***

THE WEST COAST OF AUSTRALIA

As we travelled through Coolgardie, Bullabulling, Southern Cross and various outback towns, everything became a blur through the windows of the van.

I would get up now and then from a game of snap and fish to sneak a peek, but seeing little of my surroundings as the landscape rolled past me in a blur.

I resigned myself to the fact that I could only be released from my tin cell when my captors stopped for fuel, or when they took pity on me and pulled into a truck stop so I could urinate or be fed.

There was roadworks everywhere and stretches of sealed road which made travelling a little easier, but this also meant there could be more people around.

I wasn't sure exactly where we were, as the Yugoslav tried to hide us while travelling.

Taking his time now, he zigzagged through the little outback towns. Telling our mother over a *spam sandwich,* 'I drive to Perth,' he pointed at his unfolded map. A large Western Australian map he'd purchased at one of the roadhouses. 'And go north overnight.' He ran his finger along the long highway drawn on his paper. 'This way no suspicion.'

We had avoided the big cities and driven remote tracks and unmade roads for days, but he would be compelled to enter the urban sprawl if we were to continue on our journey north.

So, we sat it out in an isolated spot and rested during the heat of the day. We played in dirt, drawing pictures with sticks and looking for pebbles to throw into the air. We played hopscotch and Chinese elastics. Robyn was good at both games, especially elastics and showed me her skills.

I tried really hard to be as talented, but after it got higher than my sisters' knees, I found it impossible to jump over the elastic, let alone jump on it.

Mum and the Yugoslav slept in the van as we children played. Skippy patiently waited and kept guard as the afternoon dragged on.

And as night descended, I slinked aboard the van with my sister creeping behind me. I was sad the freedom of the day was gone, and I would again be trapped.

My sisters and I soon fell asleep amongst the blankets and slept the night away as we travelled through Perth and out the other side.

We'd left the worst of the rough roads behind us at the border and I woke to smooth bitumen under the wheels. I had slept for hours and woke with the sun streaming in through the glass and the temperature inside stifling. Overnight we'd arrived at a little isolated water-hole not far from Geraldton.

I got to have a bath. And Skippy spent hours in and out of the watering pool, shaking his fur and spraying everyone with water more than once that day. But I couldn't blame him for I knew he felt the same as me. It was so amazing to finally feel cool and clean again.

Mother built a little fire and I watched as she boiled up some of the water from the catchment. She covered it with a tea towel and left it to cool.

'Those bloody flies are annoying,' she said as she swiped one with the fly squat she'd taken from the dash in the car, managing to squash its guts between the webbed surface. 'Got ya. I'll fill those water bottles up later, so we'll have them for drinking.' Mother was talking out loud again, speaking as she often did to no-one in particular.

I wasn't really listening. I was too busy watching her spectacle.

She waved the squat in the air, flipping and slapping it like a bad fencing demonstration. Even with her uncouth technique, she still managed to murder quite a few blowies.

It was a lovely rest and recuperation day, and the next morning I was glad to take off again along the highway.

The further north we went, the more the landscape changed, becoming flat and arid again. The orange bull dust (as it's known) was a familiar hindrance.

Yugoslav Man had slowed his driving since our departure from Geraldton, as the wildlife was always active in the area. He told us he didn't want to risk an accident. I thought it strange when the rest of his life was about risk. I suppose even criminals have some phobias.

I now sat up in the wagon beside my sisters. Mother said, 'It was far too hot to be locked up in that darn caravan.' And I nodded my head to her in agreement.

I wound down the window so I could feel the wind in my hair. Even if it was a dry warm blast full of dust, it felt heavenly.

It wasn't long before Skippy climbed over and plonked his body on my lap. He really had no manners when it came to taking turns.

I was now forced to move along the seat trying to get my sisters to move up a bit. There was the usual compliance from Rhonda, but Robyn was a different story, not happy at all to have Rhonda squish her so tightly against the opposite door.

'If you weren't so fat, we'd have more room.' Robyn spat out her insult at me.

'It's not my fault. Skippy is hogging the seat.'

'Move oo-ver.' Robyn clenched her teeth and pushed Rhonda towards me, perhaps hoping to start a chain reaction and have us slide along the vinyl bench seat.

The weight of her two siblings and a large dog were more mass than she anticipated. And with our hot sweaty thighs, we stayed glued to the seat.

Robyn showed her annoyance by insulting us and lashing out. Punching our knees.

Mother turned around and told her to stop.

Robyn was determined to show us who was the boss, and continued her onslaught. Rhonda and I yelled for her to stop.

When suddenly the Yugoslav could stand no more, he pulled off onto the shoulder of the highway.

'You're a real little bitch,' Mother said as she dragged Robyn out to rescue Rhonda.

The Yugoslav was getting really shitty. He always lost it if us girls were fighting. With Robyn always starting it, and Rhonda and me having to deal with the fallout.

Sometimes he'd explode like a hand grenade, hissing his temper and then spraying his shrapnel words to inflict his terror.

Today he threatened to leave us all in the caravan on the side of the road, which I thought was something he would probably delight in.

I tried to block him out, but his angry voice terrified me. All the while I'd be nodding like I understood, demonstrating I was paying attention. When really it was always Mother's echo that I actually heard. I still couldn't look into his eyes of steel. I just tried to blend in and shrink into the background, like I wasn't really there.

Rhonda was promoted to the front seat between him and Mother and everyone settled back as we took off. Robyn now had plenty of room and smiled with glee at her win.

Skippy leaned against the door with his head out the window blocking the space, but I didn't really mind. He was having so much fun. Besides, I expected his fur made him hotter than me.

A little later, our entourage pulled up somewhere along the coastline, for a brief reprieve. And as I opened the door, Skip and I raced from the car. He ran to lift his leg while I explored my surroundings.

Before me was a magnificent white sandy beach and a sea of clear turquoise water. Mesmerised and under its spell, I stood looking out to the ocean. But I did not swim. It was just a tourist moment with my family. And as I stared at the scenery, my eyes drank in its aura. I'd never seen anything so beautiful. A paradise from Mother Nature and a reward at the end of a punishing trip across three states.

The following days we crossed many bridges and dry creek beds. Once we reached Carnarvon, the bitumen stopped, and we were again tossed around on the dust roads of isolated communities as we headed even further north.

'In the wet season,' one of the roadhouse workers informed us, 'there is always risk of flooding. And cyclones can blow across this windy region, destroying communities. But this year it's shaping up to be short on rainfall with very little water around.'

We'd be safe from cyclones then. I really didn't like the sound of those.

***

A CARAVAN PARK IN THE PILBRA

We finally stopped and took up residence in a Port Hedland Caravan Park. Mother tried to calculate how far we'd travel by the map. 'It's hard to add up,' she said when I asked her. 'Around two thousand seven hundred miles (4,345 km) but probably more. We did have a few detours you know.'

I really loved looking at the map and working out where we'd been. Its huge printed paper was covered in coloured lines. With hundreds of names of places and a compass rose in the centre top (for directions Mother told me).

I asked her why it was missing Deniliquin where Dad lived. And why I couldn't see Geelong there either.

'It a map of only half of Australia,' Robyn butted in.

'Why only half?' I asked.

'Just because that's all we need,' Mother answered.

I didn't get it. Why did you only need half of Australia? But I let it drop and asked no more questions. I didn't want Robyn thinking she was smarter than me.

The map of *only half of Australia* was usually folded multiple times, making it small enough to put into the glovebox of a vehicle. Its edges once sharp and crisp, were now dirty and rounded from constant use. The folds starting to wear and any print on the bends had been rubbed away and replaced with thin white lines.

It was only ever opened when the Yugoslav needed it for direction, but sometimes I was allowed to unfold it and gaze at its contents. I would try to imagine what the other towns on the map looked like and wonder which ones I would visit next.

But for now, I was in Port Hedland and with my confinement over, I loved that I could run free.

The first few days we settled in and went beachcombing. I was told not to get in the water. Not till Mother knew for bloody sure if it was safe.

Mother warned us to watch for poisonous sea creatures. 'Cone fish, stone fish, box jelly fish, sea urchin and they are just a few of the small ones.' She added, 'crocodiles and sharks are in these oceans too.'

I should have been terrified, but It just made me more intrigued and ready to explore.

I was careful however not to pick up anything I thought might hurt me. And I didn't walk down along the sea because the tides took the water metres from the shore, and anyhow, I couldn't be bothered.

I loved to stroll barefoot on the tidal flats and admire the swirling patterns on its surface, squelching my toes in the little patches of warm water that glistened in the sun like mirrors. My sisters and I never wore bathers. We'd just strip off our dresses and race around in our cotton tails.

Most of Port Hedland was a bright orange hue. Everywhere I looked I saw houses, cars, and boats, all covered in bull dust. Orange rusted metal on roofs, signs and machinery. Clothing on all its people were tinged with orange. Beach cliffs and sands of orange. Even the skies above Hedland displayed their sunsets in orange.

It was just the beginning of the iron ore boom when I arrived in town, but all I knew was there were people everywhere in the park. Caravans lined up like tanks in a war zone, inhabited by the influx of workers, all there to fill the vacancies in the mining of iron ore.

There were other children in the caravan park, but I was wary of others after Mother ordered me not to talk to anyone. So, I tried to hang out with my sisters and not mix too much with others. I'd take my doll Pamela and head outside to play in the sandpit.

There was no television or radio, nothing like that in this hot orange outback town. The sandpit and playground were my main entertainment. I would sit Pamela down to watch as I dug and played beside my sisters.

Yugoslav told Mother he'd started work, but it wasn't at the mines, because Newman was nearly five hours from Port Hedland. Totally impossible for him to return home in the afternoon as he did. Perhaps he was down at the docks unloading or out at the Dampier Salt Works. I don't know and she didn't care as long as he brought in the money. But perhaps he was gambling or stealing *(which he was skilled at)* or doing a deal.

He took us all to the open-air cinema. My first Drive-In experience, and possibly the greatest. Nothing was ever quite as good as that hot night in the Pilbara with the windows wound down.

At interval we got to play on the swings and run around. I don't remember the films *(there were two),* but that wasn't the best bit anyhow. It was the joy of the new experience. A happy carefree moment in a life of bulldust.

Mother also took us to the Picture Gardens in Wedge Street a couple of times. We sat on rows of joined canvas chairs facing a big cement screen. They were fun evenings of entertainment in a town with no T.V., but it was mostly women and children attending, as the men were more entertained with drinking and gambling together.

***

A TRIP TO TOWN

Mother walked us into town one day because Yugoslav had the car. The van park was out along the road a little way. I had always walked so this seemed like nothing new. Hadn't I walked the hot roads of Deniliquin and Moree, and struggled up the hills on the iced bitumen of the highlands.

I started off keen to get going, but soon found out that this trek was to rival no other I had ever attempted before.

It was so hot, and it wasn't long before my legs grew tired and beads of sweat were running down my face. I had fair skin and couldn't stay exposed to the sun for too long or else I'd be burnt to a crisp. I had no hat, just a smear of zinc cream over the bridge of my nose. I was fully exposed to the elements that day in the Pilbara.

I started to complain as I floundered along, but I wasn't the only one. My sisters were whinging and even Mother was complaining to us about the heat. She seemed determined to push on though, and our distress only grew.

I was hotter than I could ever remember being. I tried to concentrate but my mind was playing tricks. In front of me a moving heat haze waved and floated up off the bitumen like a desert mirage. It fooled my eyes as I believed there was a lovely expanse of water up ahead. A cruel joke. Just a figment of my imagination. It grew as large as a river, a lake, and then an ocean. It looked so real, and I needed a drink. So I ran towards it. But then it was gone! Vanishing in front of my eyes. So I dragged my dehydrated self along, thirsty and boiling hot.

And then it reappeared, and I marvelled at its beauty again. And again I believed it was real. But I was smart and reasoned that it was not. It was a weird experience and one I never forgot.

By the time I arrived in town I was tired, close to exhaustion. I needed to find a tree to lie under. It wasn't just me, my siblings were exhausted too. So we lay there under a small branch. Its shadow was minimal because of the position of the sun at this time of day, but we were small and it was sufficient.

We wanted to swim in the pool, but firstly we had to rest while mother went to buy smokes and drinks. And we waited for her return. And when we were rested and hydrated, we threw off our clothes and swam in our cotton tails.

We had a good day of swimming, and then had to return to the caravan, out the road along the bitumen. We were not keen and stayed to linger in the shade of the streets.

My bum was still wet and my undies dripping, but that was good as I was still cool. The hot dusty air would dry them in no time. So I walked with a strange gait like I'd wet my pants and laughed at my sisters who were doing the same. No-one could see my wet pants though, as I was dressed. All they could see was the trickle that ran down my inside thigh.

We returned to the park. This time we were better. Our underwear acted like a cooling system, and we were totally dry by the time we reached the van. And Skippy waited tied up under the shade, excited to see us.

***

A LOST DOLL

I loved my new life. It was like being lost in a new exciting world, even if it meant *he* was here.

I never really had to talk to him much anyhow 'cause he was always working or whatever.

I had Pamela to talk to. She always understood how I felt. She'd come to court with me when I had to stand up and tell all those lies. Mum held on to her when I stood in the witness box and swore on the Bible. Pamela knew how upset I'd been, and at night we'd tell secrets about him. Pamela hated him too. She saw it all that day. The day of the fashion show, she'd watched from the bench when I'd got a drink. Yes, she knew everything.

Living here in Western Australia, there were things I had to adjust to. Like never feeling clean. And having to listen to people in the park laughing, fighting, or babbling all day. And it was a drag having to help Mother carry the washing to the laundry block. Pamela always enjoyed it though, sitting on top of the dirty wash pile.

Mother made us collect any broken pegs lying on the ground *(which was quite embarrassing)* so she could put them together later that night. Pamela had a good eye for that sort of thing, so I always took her.

The weather was always stifling, even in the middle of the night. And the dust covered everything, especially when the wind picked up. But I kinda got used to all that.

Port Hedland was just in the realms of becoming a major powerhouse to the world, but I didn't know any of that. I just loved the wildernesses and its uniqueness, and I was happy to stay forever.

I spent hours on the beaches with my sisters. Or playing with Pamela in the sandpit. It was carefree here in Port Hedland. I didn't even have to go to school. I could just enjoy the whole day playing.

But things could suddenly change without warning or explanation when you were an eight-year-old. One night we left Port Hedland. It was very sudden and unexpected. By mistake I left behind my beloved doll Pamela. I left her outside in the sandpit. And Mother wouldn't let me go and get her. I couldn't see to find her anyhow as it was pitch dark.

Mother tried to bundle me into the car like it was urgent. 'Hop in, we've gotta go.'

'But I don't wanna go! I wanna get Pamela!'

'Pamela will have to stay. She'll be okay. We can get her in the morning.' Mother sighed. 'We can't go back for her! We've got to keep going.' Mother kept repeating that.

Mother jumped in and slid across the seat next to him. 'Come on get in and shut the door before he leaves you behind as well,' Mother said in a threatening tone.

I was bawling so hard I thought I'd never stop. 'She will be lonely.' I howled climbing in. My tears flowing freely and dropping on my lap. I shut the door and left Pamela there to live forever in Port Hedland.

'It's too dark and I wouldn't find her. She has to stay,' said Mother.

'But it's not fair!' I sobbed. 'Why are we leaving? I didn't even get to say goodbye to her.' I hung my head and cried.

'Some things aren't fair!' Mother quoted.

I hated her. And I hated him. Stupid idiots, what would they know? My dolly would be lost forever.

I hoped Pamela loved Port Hedland as much as I did.

We pulled out in the darkness in the station wagon heading to who knew where?

All our possessions piled high and jammed in everywhere, so you could hardly see out the windows. Nothing seemed to be packed orderly. Instead it looked as though they had been just thrown in any old how.

We no longer had a caravan either. It stayed behind with Pamela in the park.

***

CRIMINAL BEHAVIOUR

The Yugoslav received money for the van. I don't know how much, but all profit.

'I tell Vince, it a bargain.' He told his story to Mother. They both laughed. 'He drunk, so I steal money and camera too. See! On floor down there.' He pointed to a grungy metal lunch box.

I sat in the front seat against the window today, as the back was in such disarray.

Mother bent down to claim the prize. I watched as she pulled out a flash looking camera and a pile of notes. 'It's still loaded with film, it's only on the fourth frame. Look,' she told him excitedly. But he seemed disinterested in the camera. He just wanted to see the money. She showed it to him and then put it away.

I didn't care about their stupid money. It wouldn't bring Pamela back. I wanted to sulk for the day. And when it was time to eat, I didn't want to. I was too sad.

Mother told me we were heading to Broome. Strange name. Perhaps it was where they made all the brooms. I would look at the map later to see where Broome was.

Mother wanted to stop and look at the ocean. We all jumped out to see it. But I didn't see much water. The tide had taken it so far away, all I saw was a line of blue that joined the sky.

Everything I looked at was white. But it was beautiful all the same. And I looked and I was in awe. And I thought I might have found shell heaven.

I spied millions on the beach. Lots of different shapes and colours. Small, medium and giant size. I picked up pretty sand dollars that were scattered everywhere. Their surface bleached white from the sun. Each with a pretty starfish shape patterned on their dried shell. I felt ecstatic, like I'd found all the treasure from the ocean right here on the beach. I daydreamed, maybe I could live here right beside this magical paradise. And I started to feel happy again. If only I could show Pamela.

***

INTO THE INTERIOR

We got in the car and left that beautiful beach even though I told Mum I wanted to stay. 'We've got to keep going,' she said. 'We want to get to Broome.'

But I didn't get to see much of Broome. With the Yugoslav sweating at the brow, and Mother telling him we'd better keep driving if he didn't want to get caught. 'Won't take long for them to realise their money's missing.'

So we raced on by Broome and made our way to Kununurra. And it was days before I got to look at it on the map, as it was in constant use through the Kimberly region, so I had to wait.

They took it in turns to drive. Mother said we were headed for Darwin.

When she took over the driving, she moved things around a bit and I got in the back with my siblings. Even if it was crammed, at least I didn't have to sit next to him.

As it turned out, we didn't go to Darwin. We only went as far as Kununurra at the top end.

With the road rough and tedious, it was hard going. It shook everything around in the car like a washing machine. I think he was having second thoughts of his commitment to travelling these corrugated roads.

The car was really struggling, the road more suited to a 4-wheel drive, and the wagon certainly didn't fit that description.

At least some of the scenery was spectacular with its red rock outcrops and ranges. I thought the soil looked redder here and there were definitely a few more trees. This magnificent landscape had me gazing for miles out the window. It was still hot and harsh out here, but that was what I liked about it. I knew I'd never forget it.

There were gorges too, with fresh water to wash with and boil for a cup of tea. Their rocky outcrops and cliffs screamed at me to explore them. But our visits were short and then we were gone.

The Yugoslav said there might be crocodiles in the area, but he wasn't sure. So he didn't want to hang around and get eaten. I didn't think I wanted to either.

The weather was hot and tropical with trees sparsely planted and vast expanses of grassland. A real savannah of extreme and the roads were very rough again as we made our way north east to Katherine.

I slept some of the day away with the windows all down for natural air-conditioning. It was hard not to fall asleep with the temperatures soaring by mid-morning and mother dosing us with travel medication.

There was a lot of space out there in the Kimberly and you could easily perish if you got lost. But we had our map, and in the evenings, it would come out and be studied in-depth.

We'd eat by the side of the road or park in little secluded areas. There really wasn't very much car traffic in this far north area of Australia.

I saw bottle trees (boabs) growing amongst the tussock grass in the sandy soil. To me they were the elephants of the plant world. With their thick leathery trunks and large folds, I likened it to wrinkles on the elephant, their mass humongous and their presence extraordinary.

I told Mum they were the best tree I'd ever seen. And she talked about their ability to hold water for long periods of drought. I wanted to hug them, but their massive girth made it impossible even though I tried. I asked my sister to hold hands and it was still impossible.

Their branches looked more like their roots than the top of the tree. Even at eight, I knew they were special and beautifully unique.

I didn't know where the Yugoslav was taking us, but it was full of adventure and knowledge for me. I wished Pamela could have seen all the fun I was having out here in the Kimberly outback.

I thought of her many times during the day. And then I would try not to as it made me sad.

Mother told me that she would be with a new little girl, but I wasn't convinced. I pictured her sitting in reception at the park, waiting for me to come and rescue her. And thinking she would be sad forever when I never did.

***

A DEAD BUFFALO

We'd pulled up in the dark of the night after a long day of driving in the heat and the dust.

The Yugoslav declared, 'This a wonderful place to camp. May, you get a blanket. We sleep under the stars.'

When Robyn said she wasn't sleeping out on the bloody ground, she was allowed to sleep with Rhonda in the car amongst the mess and all the gear.

So I was allotted a space beside my mother. And *he* slept alone.

After too long on the road, we were all soon asleep. Everyone exhausted and no-one even bothering to eat

Waking in the morning, we smelt an awful stench. 'What stinks!' Robyn shrieked, dry-retching as she hopped from the car.

'It's making me sick.' Rhonda held her nose, coughing and spluttering and joining the conversation. 'Yuck, it's Skippy.'

Yep it was Skippy all right. He'd decided that a dead buffalo full of maggots was just the perfume he needed today.

Little did we realise when we pulled up to our camping spot the night before, that we had in fact, fallen to sleep not 10 feet from a rotting bloated dead buffalo.

It was so pungent that everyone was feeling nauseous when we took off. Sitting in the car with that sour smell wafting across the interior was hard to deal with. But without water, we were compelled to deal with it. The Yugoslav mapped the nearest water hole.

***

ANTS

I never really thought about the ants when I looked at all the termite nests in the Kimberly. I saw them more like tall melting sandcastles. Like sculpture to be admired and photographed. I didn't think of them as an ant city. But that's what they were.

If I'd broken the nests apart, I would have been swarmed with termites ready to fight like soldiers to protect and guard their city. But I had no interest in destroying an ant home— I thought them wonderful.

We'd been travelling for over a week now through the rough red dust roads, stopping by the wayside at night to sleep.

Robyn refused to sleep out of the car, so it was me. Sometimes I got to sleep in the car when Rhonda would swap places. But mostly it was me.

Early in the morning I woke in terror. Something bug-like was crawling on me. Then I felt the biting and stinging. Like fire, it engulfed my body.

I jumped up screaming and flapped the blanket against my legs. But I couldn't stop it. And there was more pain. And it continued. I only had my cottons on, so I was covered in welts. My torso and limbs were spread with ants.

And my screaming had woken everyone. The adults, shaking off ants as well.

The Yugoslav ran for water to douse us, while my sisters were safe and sat up in the car to watch.

It was daylight anyway, so after all the ants were squished or drowned, we drove off and left that crawling campsite.

And I was miserable all day from the bites I had all over me. I had no Pamela to cuddle. So I cuddled Skippy in the back instead, until he was too hot and moved away. And then I suffered alone.

Yugoslav had chosen to camp on top of an anthill— not a termite mound, for they were harmless— but other ants that like to bite little girls who sleep out in the outback. And it was true to say I hated ants after that.

***

INTO THE CENTRE

We continued to travel many more miles (kilometres) through the changing landscape heading south from Katherine to Alice Springs in the middle of Australia.

We were nearly into the centre of the country when an ambulance flew by, smashing our windscreen. The stones on the road hit the glass and it smashed into little pieces.

The Yugoslav knocked the shards out onto the side of the road. The edges he left intact stuck in the rubber. Now we could frame the scenery through a frosted frame.

Mother said it was a real hindrance and she didn't want to drive, which just seemed to make the Yugoslav all the more determined to get out of the outback faster. He said it was a nightmare, but I could tell him what a nightmare was really about. Fat and skinny men and raging rivers. But I shut up and let him rant.

It took a bit of cleaning to rid the seats and floors of shards of glass. Some having found their way into little obscure places, which became very bothersome for anyone sitting in the front. So my sisters and I preferred to stay in the back seat. No risk of a glass injury that way.

The Yugoslav was driving erratically and not slowing down at all over the cracks and holes in the road. His impatience ensured we were bounced around.

In the centre of Australia, the arid environment guaranteed the weather was hot and dry. Without a windscreen, it was blasting in like a hairdryer on full heat. With all the windows down, it at least escaped out the sides a little.

He started complaining to Mother as it blasted his face, his patience wearing thin and his demeanour tense.

'My new wagon is a bloody mess,' cried Mother, now seemingly upset with the whole situation.

I nodded, as I had to agree.

The Yugoslav lost it. Telling her to be quiet. 'I doing my best. We get it fixed soon.'

Tensions remained high as the bull dust blasted in and coated everything, including us.

We blew another tyre just to add to our misery. Lucky for the Yugoslav, he'd replaced the spare with a new one back in Port Hedland.

Even more lucky was the fact that given the way he was driving, we weren't injured.

We all got out while he changed it.

'It's a good time to eat. It might stop you fighting in the back,' Mother said.

I wanted to tell her I had my doubts.

Robyn had started pushing us around, trying to get the best position for minimal dust, which was ridiculous because you couldn't get away from it anyhow. But she was skilled at causing arguments.

After a quick snack, it did in fact put everyone in a better mood as we continued on. And puncturing another tyre sure slowed the Yugoslav down. Becoming a little more cautious with his driving again, put everyone at ease.

'With the spare in shreds, it wouldn't pay to be too reckless,' Mother told him gingerly.

The windscreen became a real problem, with every flying bug in the Northern Territory it seemed, wanting to take a ride in our vehicle.

It was like a game of chicken. Those that didn't make it, splattered on the bumper and headlights.

Bug guts thick and dry stuck like cement. The survivors managed to fly aboard and enjoy their reign of terror on the stupid mammals, enjoying our squeals and shivers, laughing as we got ourselves into a right old state.

Skippy managed to devour the smart-arse ones that paraded in front of him. And I praised him for his bravery.

'Ewww, what are they? Get them out,' Rhonda said, trying to flick them out, but without much success.

Mother said, 'Be quiet!'

And the Yugoslav said, 'Stop being stupid. I get car windscreen fixed as soon as I can.' He pointed. 'That's Ayer's Rock somewhere over there.'

I didn't know what he meant. But we didn't stop to see it anyway. No time because we needed to get the windscreen fixed.

He drove into Alice Springs and hung around while he organised the windscreen. It took a while, but we sat in the shade and played, and we waited. And soon we were underway.

Checking the map wasn't any good anymore, as we only had half of Australia. 'We are over the edge, in the middle,' Mother said.

Now I wished we had all of Australia, then I could check how far we were from home. But where was home? Somehow, I didn't think we had a home anymore. And that made me think of Pamela. I wondered did she have a home. And then I was sad again.

I sat and stayed quiet. The pain of always leaving behind everything I loved gashed like a wound in my heart. Always picking up the pieces of my scattered life tired my soul and chipped away at my self-esteem. Like I didn't matter. I had to look after me for only I would.

It was good not to have bugs. I slept.

***

A KANGAROO JOEY

I could see their all-wheel drive had minimal damage as we pulled up alongside them. The mother kangaroo lay dead on the road.

'The front bumper has taken much of the impact,' the young guy said to the Yugoslav through the window of the car.

I found that hard to believe! It looked to me like the kangaroo took most of the impact. Her poor carcass spattered with blood and a stream of red running from her nose. They had dragged her off to the side of the road where she lay on her side in an unnatural position.

Skippy whimpered, wanting to escape for a look.

'Would you folks be interested in looking after a baby kangaroo? Her mother jumped out onto the road in front of us and we couldn't stop. Money's short so if you give us five dollars, she's yours,' he said.

Mother had a soft heart when it came to rescuing animals and she could not bear to walk away. With us harping in the back and mother in the front, together, we convinced the Yugoslav. And the deal was done.

All of us were instantly smitten by her cute little joey face. She stayed wrapped in cloth to keep her warm and snug. They named her Skippy (Number Two). I thought it ridiculous. But Skippy Two she remained.

Skip the dog was very interested, and soon became accustomed to his new car buddy. Sticking his nose in there, he sniffed the little creature often just to check she was okay.

And that orphaned baby Joey slept cosy in the car and joined our family crammed in like the rest of us.

**

DIG FOR WATER

Trouble was just down the road.

The car was a mess. Not only the exterior dirt and grime, or the dust-covered seats and floor, but the engine, the wheels and the body were feeling the strain.

I was a little worried when our wagon finally broke. I didn't know what was wrong, but it was serious, and we had no choice but to stay put.

'I have to go find help to fix car. You stay with girls. I be back soon.' The Yugoslav left us.

He started to walk forward along the road, and I watched him as he faded into the distance.

Us females waited with the car like we had been instructed.

It was mid-morning when he left us and by lunchtime the heat was becoming unbearable.

There was nowhere to sit other than the scorching vinyl seats. Mother said to throw the blankets over them. I tried to stay still because she said that would stop us feeling so thirsty. But the sun streaming through the glass intensified the heat and there was very little shade.

Skippy Dog hadn't moved from under the car for hours. But his relentless panting assured me that he was still alive.

We had placed the kangaroo beside Skippy Dog in a bid to protect her from exposure to the sun as well.

Our joey had been born into this harsh environment.

Mother had fed her earlier with a bottle of milk, but now there was no water, and we were all at the mercy of the weather and our situation.

I started whining and complaining about something to drink, my thirst the only thing I could focus on. Robyn and Rhonda joined in too.

After constant nagging, Mother suggested we dig for water.

We sat down on the boiling sandy soil. Together we dug with our hands, frantically at first. I dived my eight fingers into the scalding earth. Flicking the particles of sand and dust to the side of me. My sisters mirrored the task. Skippy had seen the fun and now joined us with a gusto of energy.

We were optimistic at first, deciding together if we got up on our knees, we could lever out more sand from the dent we had created. We were making a little hole. But the land was hard from lack of moisture, I retrieved the shears (I always knew where to find them) and stabbed them into the earth to continue the dig. My fingers were sore and damaged from the heat and the coarse dry dirt and perhaps the shears would do the trick.

We tried a while longer, Mother joining us. But it was useless. Even the shears couldn't penetrate further and digging only succeeded in making us exhausted and stressed. I discarded the shears where I sat.

I started seeing mirages again like I had in Port Hedland. This time I enjoyed the folly. It was somehow comforting and familiar.

Blue shimmers of cool water lapped in the distance. I could lie down and let it wash over me. If I closed my eyes, I could sleep, and the sun would take me to heaven. I was sure the Yugoslav had left us to dehydrate and die out here in this desert environment. Maybe he had passed away himself on his expedition to the mechanic's.

I wanted to give up the fight. Without water, I was done. My mind started to wander as I stared into the void, by the edge of the small concave in the ground.

My sisters beside me also struggled. Robyn still chipped away at the soil with a butter knife she'd found amongst our belongings. Her resilience and sheer determination, a survival tactic born out of necessity, meant she would not give up.

Rhonda had stopped digging but supported Robyn's continued efforts alongside her.

Through my hazed mind, I thought I saw a blue Combi van with people. Dressed in flowing rags of colour and beads of glaze and wood, matted windswept hair and smiles like sunbeams of love.

'Hello there!' said the voice of a stranger. 'What are you all digging for? Can we help you?'

'Water! We are all digging for water. We ran out this morning when my husband walked off to get help. And we are very thirsty. He has not come back yet,' explained mother.

'We have spare water. You can have some of ours,' they kindly said. 'And we will look out for him along the road and tell him of your troubles. If we do not find him, we will send someone back to rescue you all.'

True to their word, they handed us a container of water. Wished us well and drove off.

The water was heavenly. I gulped it down, not even considering the rest of my family. The liquid moistened my parched lips and throat. I wanted to scull the entire contents. But mother stopped me, then handed it on to Rhonda. And I was forced to share.

It saved our lives. I am sure of that.

The Yugoslav said his late return was made quicker by the generosity of the hippies in the van.

Our wagon was towed away for repairs. We remained for a couple of days before we again headed along the highway towards Victoria.

Our outback breakdown had been a near-death experience.
***

PART FOUR:
FINDING SOMEWHERE TO LIVE

AN EVICTION

Back in Melbourne, one morning after driving the Yugoslav to work at his new job with the brewery, we found our possessions discarded on the nature strip of the white weatherboard we rented. And the landlord had secured the house so we could not enter.

I was curious as to what was going on. While Mother was furious and panicked.

We found our blankets and kitchenware clumped in a heap on the grass. Rhonda and Robyn's favourite dolls sat on the pile looking stunned at the passing traffic.

Pamela of course missed out on all the adventure. She would have enjoyed her morning watching the busy commute of city workers.

We got out and helped Mother throw the remains of our lives into the back of the wagon and we headed for Aunt Virginia's.

***

A FLAT

Mother got a job at the chocolate factory and we moved to Northcote, in a shopping precinct.

I liked the new flat we moved into. It was around the corner behind the shops. Its exterior was made from smooth orange bricks and the Yugoslav even had a roller door garage to hide the wagon. It came furnished, with nice pieces of furniture and felt homey straight away.

I loved that it was private in behind the fence. No-one could see me there. But if I climbed the stairs to the outside balcony, and looked over the wall, I could certainly see them.

I loved to play up there with my sisters. And Mother said she loved it too.

'You girls make too much mess. At least up there I can't see it,' she said.

Mess! I scoffed at her assumption. I didn't think we made much mess. In fact, I wanted to tell her that she and the Yugoslav made much more mess than us children.

The little bathroom was crowded with beauty products of excessive amounts. Razors, deodorants, shampoos and perfume. For him and for her.

Beer bottles overflowed from the bin. And the cigarette butts squashed in odd shapes filled the ashtrays and littered the nest of tables in the lounge area. *Mess! They were the messy ones.*

The adults made us wash the dishes, sweep the floors and empty those ashtrays. I didn't think our mess should worry her, because the responsibility for cleaning it would certainly fall on us anyhow.

They enrolled me in school. And I was shown the safest route to walk every morning. 'Just reverse it going home,' Mother said.

Today she sent me out the door with a packed sandwich *(which I knew I wouldn't eat)* in a brown paper bag. I waved her goodbye and followed my sisters.

'I will see you all just after five,' Mother called out after us.

It was a cold overcast day and we ran home after school just to keep warm.

I was impatient to see our baby kangaroo. She always seemed happy to see us. And I knew she would be hungry today as it was more than a little cold.

As Robyn unlocked the door and we raced inside. Baby Skippy Joey's furry grey ears began to twitch. They were always the first thing I saw sticking out from her blankets. And to feel them gave me a good indication of her temperature.

Today as I stroked the length of them, I knew she was freezing. Her little body seemed smaller somehow as she hunched in her wrap.

Robyn went to mix the formula. She was very grown up and was often left in charge of everyone.

I went hunting for clean rags to change Skippy Joey. Her coldness worried me. We'd been told to keep her warm. After all, Mother had warned us that she came from the desert.

But Melbourne was nowhere near the desert. In fact, now that winter was in full swing, Melbourne was more like an ice region. I worried that she would not survive.

Rhonda moved Skippy Joey's box over near the little bar heater, while Robyn turned it on. We sat with the joey as she drank her bottle. She nuzzled her pretty little face against ours and she filled our hearts with love.

'Let's go and play,' said my sisters heading out the door.

'Baby Skippy Joey is going to sleep. Yeah let's,' I answered, running out behind them.

We scampered up to the balcony with Skippy Dog right behind. Mastering the steps skilfully.

I missed travelling in the car with him. Snuggled up on the back seat with the temperature scorching. I missed his funny bug-catching antics when we'd lost our windscreen. I even realised I missed all his stinking buffalo perfume. What a character our travelling dog was.

I'm sure Skippy missed it too. Having found himself resigned to a boring backyard life, his outback adventures now over.

The balcony was our stage. Performing our concerts in front of our pretend audience. I loved how they sighed and clapped at our beautiful singing.

Rhonda was bored and preferred to practise her skipping skills with her new rope.

As the cloud closed in and the sun disappeared, it got really cold. And I wanted to go inside and watch the telly.

Only problem was that I couldn't. Robyn had left the key to the door inside on the bench. I really wasn't happy. But neither was anyone else. Mother would be at least another half an hour. So we waited in the cold and there was nothing else we could do. Poor Skippy Joey was burning by the radiator as we played. If Mother had been just a little later, she'd have been in flames.

As I unlocked the door, my nostrils filled with the smell of singed fur. We were all panicked when we saw baby Skippy Joey beside the radiator.

'Turn off the heater quick!' called Mother. As she picked up the joey, rescuing her from her smouldering bed. 'What the hell were you girls doing? You could have burnt the whole flat down.'

How bad did we feel for poor Skippy Joey? Her blankets were singed, and a patch of fur had turned yellow and scorched. Thankfully she was okay, and we had saved her just in time.

A few weeks later Mother brought home chocolate buddies from the factory where she worked. She hid them in the sideboard cupboard in the lounge. Buddies of all colours were too tempting for us. Like treasure. We hunted. And couldn't leave them alone.

Rhonda thought it would be a nice gesture to offer them around one night when Mother's boss came to visit. Rhonda was like that. Generous and always willing to share.

But Mother wasn't happy, and when they left, Mother yelled at Rhonda and slapped her legs. I hadn't seen May this mad for ages. And it puzzled me what Rhonda had done. Five finger discounts obtained from your boss's business wasn't usually appreciated, and I think May might have just lost her job that night. Or maybe the Yugoslav was in trouble again. Whatever it was, we left Northcote and our homey flat with the balcony and moved to Ocean Grove.

***

A BEACH HOUSE AND A FRIEND

Running from the law was exhausting. I had no idea why my parent was zigzagging across Australia, but it was hard to keep up with. A multitude of homes discarded like rubbish. My life an endless cycle of disruption. And a corrosion of family stability.

Our new house was a bit dingy; its interior walls painted in semi-gloss paint in strange colours, like left over shades mixed together to make enough to coat the walls. Every room had a different strange combination. A stale musty smell of being locked up for too long hit my nostrils, and old used grungy furniture occupied its rooms.

Though certainly not as homey as our Melbourne flat, at least we could have the freedom to walk to the beach.

The house belonged to Bill. Mother met Bill when we were living in the blue house last year. Back then she owned an old Holden. It was so old that one day it broke down in the traffic.

'Stay here, don't leave the car, and keep the doors locked,' Mother said.

'Where are you going?' I asked, grimacing and frowning at the thought. *Why was she leaving us alone?*

She'd manage to pull the wreck off the road a little, before ripping on the hand brake. The vehicle had stopped dead on a steep incline. 'Oh shit, stay in the car! Don't move. And for God's sake don't play with the hand brake or you'll roll down the hill. I'll be back. I'm going for help.' She got out and took off along the road, with the traffic whizzing past her.

Robyn sat staring at the handbrake with a look of horror plastered on her face. Without turning to look, she ordered us to stay still and not to move.

Mother really didn't need to warn me. I'd heard what she had said and I was terrified. I could hear my shallow breathing as I tried to keep as still as I could. The minutes passed slowly. Like a game of statues, we sat transfixed to the seats. Nobody wanting to be the first to move.

It felt like a lifetime — sitting, waiting, breathing. I went over it in my head. Over and over. *Sitting, waiting, breathing.* And I prayed for her to return soon.

When she did return, she'd brought Bill with her. I let out a sigh of relief. Poor Robyn was so angry, she instantly voiced her objection at being put in such a precarious situation. Mother, however, did not respond to her objections at all and just continued her conversation with Bill. I sat in the back wondering, *did she even understand how traumatised she had made us? Maybe not.* Bill went about tying a rope to the front of our car, and when he had finished, Mother jumped back in beside Robyn.

Placing her car in neutral, Mother slowly released the handbrake. The car recoiled backwards before the rope took up the slack. Robyn visibly shook and refused to open her eyes until we were safely back in Bill's garage. And now here we were staying in her friend's holiday house in Ocean Grove. I didn't know if it was a coincidence or not, but Bill lived in Bell Park as had the Yugoslav. Sometimes I used to think that maybe, just maybe, they were all interwoven somehow.

I really liked Bill even though he was old. I hadn't really had a loving grandfather. My mother kind of adopted him.

He already had grown up children and a hoard of grandchildren, but that didn't matter. He seemed happy to just slip mother and us girls into his life.

When we arrived in Ocean Grove and allowed the freedom to explore and roam. The safe quiet little community was within walking distance of the beach. Mother had warned us not to swim out very far in the water. 'It doesn't have poisonous fish like Port Hedland, but it has a dangerous undertow. So be careful or you will drown.'

I could see the warning signs posted at various locations along the beach, so I knew mother was telling the truth. Due to that, I mostly paddled out to the height of my thighs, just to be certain. I was like that. Never daring to do too much. I needed to play it on the safe side, as the rest of my life was so stressful and out of my control, that when I got the chance to make a decision, I always chose the secure option.

The shops were close to the beach and I loved buying hot chips on our way home after a swim. Each of us paying separately and having our own wrapped parcel. By tearing the top open and eating a chip one at a time, they would last the whole walk home.

I was always happy by the beach. Sand and waves had a calming effect on my hectic turbulent life. I never had anyone to talk to about my fears and anxieties. Mother was too wrapped up in her own nightmare and my father was never around. I loved seeing my father, but I did wonder if he would have bothered with us if Mother hadn't taken us to see him all our lives.

And my sisters? Well they were in the same situation. I was so happy to have them in my life. I couldn't have gone through all this turmoil without them.

Baby Skippy Joey made it to the seaside, but she was sick. Even when she got to eating the grass in the yard, we could not clear up her scours. Then one day our beautiful precious baby joey died.

We all cried, and I was upset for weeks. And she is buried there in the corner of the yard at the seaside, sleeping and forever listening to the tides roll in and reseed.

PART FIVE:
THE HOMES

TAKEN AWAY

The Yugoslav had disappeared. I didn't know what was happening, but I felt sure he was gone for good. Mother didn't explain his disappearance, but then perhaps I didn't care to know.

It was over for good, and there was only the four of us again. I wanted to scream it from the rooftops. *He's gone. Yippee, he's gone! And he's never coming back.*

But the car went too. Repossessed was the word my mother used. I wasn't sure what that meant, but I was sure it was bad. Without a car we weren't going anywhere, I guessed.

So, I just enjoyed the sunshine and the warming of the sand as summer approached. I played ball in the yard. Drew hopscotch on the paths. And on the days when the sun wasn't shining, I'd build card houses, or make cubbies over the chairs. Ocean Grove felt like one big seaside holiday.

My sisters and I loved to go down to the beach whenever we could. Skippy Dog enjoyed the adventure and would run ahead as we made our way. Bounding into the waves on arrival and rolling in the sand, Skip loved his new neighbourhood.

Last weekend we'd gone to paddle in the waves and run on the sand with the dog.

Walking along the dirt roads barefoot had been a little hard on my feet, but there'd been plenty of cool Cooch grass to walk on in the front of the houses along the way. I could relieve them in seconds by just standing on that cool cushioned grass.

Sometimes I'd wear shoes in the warmer months but mostly I loved to go barefoot at the beach and feel the grainy sand under my feet. Besides it was a real nuisance to have to carry them everywhere. I'd opt for none.

We'd had a lovely couple of hours wandering around and exploring. Hunting up and down the shoreline for treasures, Rhonda found a couple of stones to decorate our sandcastles. We dug deep moats to surround them. I'd brought a small bucket from home to fill them with salt water.

Telling mother later when I got home, she said we could do it again next weekend if we liked.

But as it turned out, I was to be disappointed, because Mother went to hospital. And it was serious.

It was just an ordinary school day in November, but that day was Friday which made me excited as the following day I could go to the beach like Mum said.

Our school was just across the road so we'd had a competition this morning as to who could skip the fastest and arrive first.

Robyn won as she had the longest legs. And Rhonda wasn't far behind her. That meant I was last. But that's how it usually went anyhow. I was more like the Shetland and they were more like the Arab.

I'd been learning many new words and really enjoyed my spelling. Moving house all the time meant I had missed lots of schooling. It had been hard the last few months as I tried hard to catch up. I practised my spelling every day and was very proud of how well I was doing.

Mother never really took an interest in my schoolwork, but that never stopped me from trying really hard. I never saw her as my tutor. Every milestone in my life was made by me, and I was very capable and independent.

They weren't just three- and four-letter words now for grade two, but big long words like beautiful, because and children. The best thing about school was having new friends and playing games. I decided to wear shorts to school so I could hang upside down and not show my undies. I was getting older now and I didn't like the boys staring and making fun of me.

I loved playing in the girl groups. Skipping with long ropes or jumping elastics. And any spare moment I had, I joined in clapping hands and rhyming in pairs.

After lunch the lady from the office took me from my classroom and escorted me to the principal's office.

I hadn't been naughty so I wasn't fearful, just a little curious as to why the principal would want to see me. I approached the reception area.

Two police officers stepped out from behind the principal's office door.

'Oh.' I cringed with regret. *What now?*

In my short life I had seen too many police officers already. My momentary glance told me something bad was about to happen.

'It's okay, we will clarify everything once we get into the car.' *Car! Did she mean the police car?* I was trying to process what she was saying, as the muddle of adult talk and sympathetic looks made me nauseous.

Only now did I notice my eldest sister Robyn standing in the hall alongside me. With her gob opened and a look of horror on her face, I could see she, too, was not feeling well.

'Your mother's sick, and we've taken her to hospital.'

Hospital. Did I hear her say hospital? Mother was okay this morning. Wasn't she? I tried to remember. In my confused state nothing was clear. *Come to think of it, she was still in her nightie and she wasn't very cheerful. I couldn't imagine however that she was so sick as to end up in hospital.*

Teaching staff were trying to gather us into a huddle. *Probably to hand us over with minimal fuss.*

Rhonda arrived into the huddle as they ushered us towards the door. 'Come on! You're all here now. Let's go.'

The navy uniformed females looked very official. Taking charge, they scuttled us out of the building, through the school gate and into their parked vehicle.

'Where are you taking us?' Robyn whined.

'We'll take you to the station until we find somewhere safe for you all to go. You can't stay at home by yourselves while your mother's in hospital,' the cop said.

None of us knew what was really happening. Usually Robyn was not so easily accepting of strangers telling her what to do. But today was different, this was something she had no say in.

Feeling like criminals, we were escorted to the police station and sat on a bench to wait.

I had visited a police station before in stressful circumstances, so my anxiety at revisiting and enduring more police presence was overwhelming.

As I sat pondering my past visit, it conjured up all my pent-up emotions of guilt and shame that I had not forgotten. I shuddered at the thought.

When they came to speak quietly to me, I was incoherent.

'Are you hungry? Do you want something to eat?'

My answer was staggered and not making sense. And I was glad when my sisters answered, 'Yes, we are.'

***

MAY IS SICK

Earlier that day…

The breakfast dishes sitting in the sink had not been washed. Toast crumbs had dried and stuck to the plate surfaces. Dregs of milk residue sat in little slicks in the plastic cereal bowls. Mother's half-drunk cup of tea sat on the bench. May didn't feel like washing them. They were the last thing on her mind.

She still wore her dressing gown and nightie. She hadn't bothered to get dressed earlier while the girls were home.

Darkness enfolded her and she couldn't shake the feeling of doom. Life always smashed into her and knocked her off her feet. Getting up on her feet again seemed impossible. Years of disappointment had taken their toll. Today was the day she'd end it all for good.

Bill was evicting her from his seaside rental. She knew Bill wasn't heartless. He'd given her prior warning that he needed to rent his bungalow this holiday season to subsidise his income. But where would she go?

She had no vehicle, no job, no man to bring in an income. So she had just stayed. And now it was time to go. But she didn't want to struggle anymore. It was too hard. Her children deserved more than she could give them. She was always making the wrong choices. She knew they would be much better off without her.

She tried to rationalise her decision as she climbed back into her bed. *I mustn't worry, it will all turn out.* Her tears flowed over the pillow. A life of terror, deceit, and lies, that's what she'd endured. She didn't want it anymore.

The only thing she loved in the world were her girls. But they were suffering, and she couldn't look after them. She was a failure who should die. The voices told her to just be done with it.

It took some time, but as the medication dispersed through her system, she closed her eyes and drifted away.

She hadn't been lying down long when she heard a faint voice call out. But she was now flying through the clouds. Maybe she'd dreamed it and it was just the voices following her to God.

Small white doves cooed as they foraged, and beams of coloured light bounced on cumulus clouds.

Choirs of children sang in harmonised voices. Their sound following as she floated along.

There it was again. This time louder and more urgent.

'Wake up!'

She tried to block the sound and continue her journey, not wanting to wake from her heavenly place.

'Wake up! May!'

It's barely audible.

'May what have you taken?'

Someone was shaking her.

Oh, why wouldn't they just leave her alone?

Suddenly her doves startled and took flight. And her choir stopped.

Why were they shaking her from her peaceful slumber? And why was she so cold?

'Wake up, May! You have to wake up!'

May opened one eye. Very slowly at first. Her lids felt heavy. Like someone had glued them tightly shut. She closed it again, just wanting to stay in her slumber forever.

But now he was pulling her upright in the bed and throwing off her blankets.

She was still very woozy and collapsed back on the bed. He was now getting upset with her it seemed. She didn't like being ordered around.

Opening both eyes, she tried to focus. Bill. Shock rolled through her. *What was he doing here? And why was he trying to get her up out of bed?*

He pulled her to an upright position again and started slapping her on the cheeks. She was forced to voice her displeasure at his annoyance. But she couldn't manage more than a few slurred words.

Did she really utter that garbage? She tried again, but it was useless. Closing her eyes again, she swayed as he held her firmly in a sitting position. Her stomach roiled. Slowly the event came flooding back in her mind. And then she vomited.

He'd seen it coming and had managed to lift the blankets to her mouth. As she convulsed what seemed like buckets of spew, he continued to watch over her patiently until she'd ceased her spasms.

He insisted on taking her to the bathroom for a clean-up. 'How many of those pills did you take? I need to take you to the hospital.'

May didn't want to go to the hospital. She wasn't ready to have them dictate and recite her problems back to her.

He led her to the bathroom and she let him. He filled the basin and sat her down on the fluffy stool that usually sat in the corner of the room. After handing her a flannel, he left her to wash and pulled the door.

Bill stayed with her for most of the morning as she tried to work out what to do. She wasn't really making a lot of sense, but he was patient and a good listener.

When she was ready, Bill wanted to take her to the hospital, but May insisted he drive her to the police station.

Her hair must be a mess as she hadn't dried it after her bath. Her clothes were a little crumpled up. That didn't bother her too much. It was the embarrassment of what she'd done that worried her more.

She knew she needed help and he was here to take her. *Thank goodness for Bill. He was a real friend.*

On the drive to Geelong, she could hardly stay awake, so Bill turned up the radio real loud and opened his window. Numb, unable to speak, she sat in silence.

Inside the station, they were shown to a quiet room and waited patiently to see someone.

The officers assigned to see her were very nice. She was so messed up, she was blurting out sentences that weren't making sense, stopping and starting her story as she sniffled and blubbered away.

They were used to listening to sob stories and kept their composure. May appreciated their patience and concern, not seeming to judge her on her behaviour. She felt able to tell them the truth.

'I can't look after my girls properly. I have no money. I have a mental disorder that needs treatment. It's just not fair on my children.' May cried and let it all out.

'Go to the hospital,' the younger officer said, nodding his reassurance. 'We can place your children into care until you are well enough to provide for them.'

'There are procedures we can put into place.' The female officer held compassion in her eyes. 'You don't need to worry. They will be well looked after.'

They seemed genuinely caring. May believed what they were telling her. She had to.

The thread of web that had been holding her together was now broken and in tatters. And she did not have the strength to hang on to it. She had to let go.

***

WITHOUT OUR MOTHER

When I saw myself as a child, I imagined that I was clean and tidy. But how would I know, when I was young. I had no standards only the ones set for me. My family travelled in a dusty dirty station wagon, across the harsh outback of Australia, with very little water to wash in.

Did we look neglected and bedraggled? Maybe May's breakdown had been brewing for a while. In the photographs (and there were many) my sisters and I were immaculate. I don't think they painted the full picture.

There had always been Mother. I had never been without her. Even through all the domestic arguments, when my father had been out of control with his drunken tempers, she had gathered us all together for protection.

As we tramped from place to place and the times were unbearable, she had never left my side. And today she was gone from my life. Not a kiss or wave good-bye. No reassurance that all would be well. Just gone.

All I had was vague information from uniformed robots. All programmed with the same information. 'Your mother's ill and she's gone to hospital. She can't look after you.'

Everyone was being really kind to me, smiling a forced smile. Maybe they felt sorry for the three little homeless girls with useless parents. They'd seen it many times before, I was sure.

I just wanted to go home.

And where was poor Skippy. My heart tore as I thought of him alone pining for us.

Later in the day, the police drove us to Melbourne. I got in the middle and my sisters either side. After a harrowing day, I managed to doze off a little on the way. The CB radio crackled and continuously hissed in the front with voices cutting in and out.

Arriving at the city cop shop, I was asked to wait again. I really didn't want to wait anymore. My bum was numb from sitting around. Today Robyn was on her best behaviour and hadn't antagonised me a bit. Maybe I could get her going? They might lock her up.

I knew I wouldn't, though. Remember, I always played it safe.

After dark, they got the word and we were off to Allambie in Burwood.

***

ALLAMBIE

Allambie was described as a treatment, classification and transit centre for Wards of the State, which was an accurate description. In the seventies, the centre accommodated up to ninety children between the ages of two and fourteen. The social worker told us that this was usually only a short-term solution until children were either returned to their families or moved to other facilities in the state.

We arrived in the darkness of night.

Even after a harrowing, exhausting day, I was still having to meet adults and listen to them babble on. What had started off as an ordinary school day had turned into a nightmare.

The staff were fluffing over paperwork as we stood huddled together with the police officers.

The cops said their goodbyes when the handover was completed and gave waves like hand signals to us on departure. They were actually really nice and made me feel a little better.

I didn't take much notice of what was going on. It was all a little overwhelming and I was very nervous arriving in a strange building with strangers.

'Everyone's in bed. We're just waiting to see if we can find somewhere for you girls to sleep tonight. And tomorrow we'll sort out a permanent bed for you all.'

I didn't care. I was so tired and lost, I just wanted to lay my head on a pillow and forget today had ever happened.

The halls were quiet as we made our way through the building. It was dimly lit and hard to navigate. Keeping up was difficult. I couldn't ever remember having been up so late and I was sure I was going to collapse if I didn't lie down soon.

After arriving at a large room, in order to create minimum disturbance, they didn't turn on the lights.

I tried to adapt my eyes to the space, which was impossible as it was pitch dark in there.

'You girls can bunk together tonight,' our charge whispered, pointing to a void in the dark.

Moving forward a little, my foot bumped the side of mattress which was on the floor.

'Here, lie down,' she said, bending down to turn back the bedding.

I didn't need to be asked again and slid in quickly. My sisters followed my lead and we were in.

Then the staff member turned and left as we snuggled in the blankets. No-one acknowledged our presence which suited me fine, as I rolled over in readiness for sleep.

Only not everyone was asleep and soon the whispers started. Their talk was of a sexual nature. Girls obviously older than me and had troubled lives.

Lying inconspicuously in the dark, I listened, (as did my sisters) to the whispered stories from faces I couldn't see. Hearing tales of sordid teenage lives that night. I tried to stay awake to hear the gossip, but exhaustion made it impossible and I slipped into slumber.

The following days were a bit of a blur as the full impact took its toll on me. How did we get here in this cattle yard for children?

The days ran into each other, spinning crazily in my head, as I tried to make sense of it all. It was a fun game if you didn't crash. Take the ride of your life. Be careful, though, you never know what's around the corner.

I had a new life, and for the most part I approached it with positivity. Attending school at the centre filled my days. With lots of kids to play with, the days went quickly.

Like a prison full of children, there were daily line ups for clean clothes and showers. We were given health check-ups and daily chores to do.

With little information on my family, I was listed as no fixed address and my father's whereabouts as unknown. That never stopped them injecting me with diseases in the name of immunity even if I'd already suffered most of them.

When it came to Robyn's turn to be jabbed, she was having none of it. All their sweet talking made no difference. She was petrified and let out a piecing scream. I heard her use the "b" word as well as the "f" word.

Robyn could swear better than anyone else I knew. She used it as a fighting mechanism. It was her power over everyone. With adults, it often got her the attention, and with me and Rhonda it usually resulted in her getting what she wanted.

The nurses weren't impressed by Robyn's behaviour. It only seemed to make them more determined to jab her. It took two to drag her off and hold her down.

It was hard to watch, and I felt sorry for her. No-one gave them permission to traumatise her this way. It was all a little crazy really.

Her shoe came off and hit a nurse as she struggled to break free. But they were stronger, and she was outnumbered. As the needle penetrated her flesh, she let out a blood-curdling scream. It was over; she collapsed and slid down the wall.

Overcrowding in Allambie meant we had to be moved to a new facility. I had been here for just over a month and today I was leaving.

On my departure, I was issued with a new suitcase. In it was all I owned. Three pretty new dresses, a cardigan, some new cotton tails and some lovely white socks and a pair of lace ups. I had never owned a suitcase before. It made me feel important and privileged for once in my life.

***

BLACK HALL MANSION
(The Catherine Booth Girls Home)

It was a week after my ninth birthday. My celebration forgotten. Perhaps in fact it was hushed up and never acknowledged. I cannot be sure, for it was erased or buried deep within my brain.

Today was my leaving day. I had feelings of excitement at being moved to somewhere less crowded. My feelings were hard to contain as I waited patiently for the process to be finalised. Maybe my new home would be better. Allambie was chaos.

I struggled to cope with the sudden separation and disappearance of my mother. I pined for her and cried at nights for Skippy. They were in my prayers as I knelt at bedtime and spoke to God. Not knowing their whereabouts left me with feelings of anxiety and loss. Like a crime had been committed but no-one was accountable. My loved ones disappeared without a trace. No-one saw that I had shut down myself for protection.

I felt lonely in my thoughts. Keeping feelings inside me was my way of coping. I wouldn't allow myself to lose control. Instead, I had to work it out and try to heal myself. I had no-one to talk to anyhow. Who would listen?

My dreams of Pamela nearly drove me to insanity. Like me, she was lost. We had to cope alone. My only comforts were the faces of my sisters. They were the threads to my past— the only things I recognised.

The relief today of leaving this crazy sorting facility to a new home, gave me hope.

As I waved my fellow prisoners goodbye, I wished them luck for a happy life. My sisters also said their goodbyes and would accompany me to our new accommodation.

I had a good feeling about the move as I neared my destination. The houses in this area resembled mansions from story books. The lush ambiance instantly appealed to me as the vehicle entered the Ward.

I had not visited this part of Melbourne before and I was astounded at the magnificent historic trees that grew here. Their aged branches spread wide to shade the roads with dappled light. Many elaborate houses of the neighbourhood were set way back off the streets. Some stood proud in full view as we drove past. While others peeked out from behind the foliage that encased their gardens.

On arrival through the entranceway of Blackhall, the splendour of my new home amazed me. The grandeur of its Italianate architecture took my breath away. I couldn't believe this was where I would live. Maybe I was dreaming, but I hoped that I wasn't.

There were children obviously enjoying their afternoon as they created a massive castle in the sand beside the building. I waved at them and they yelled out hello which was very welcoming. As we pulled up a little further on and stopped, I thought to myself that I might like to join them later on. And today I was happy.

As it turns out, it was a busy place, full of noisy girls. Mealtimes were cloned portions of chow eaten at tables side by side. We recited grace before every meal and said our prayers at bedtime.

They spoke of God in punishment and in triumph. God didn't like idle hands, so I kept mine busy. And hygiene was crucial, as "Cleanliness is next to *Godliness*". And who wanted to be a dirty devil.

I never had fights with the other girls, with the one exception, of course, my sisters, but that was to be expected.

***

UNJUST PUNISHMENT

They took us in for a hurried meeting with the Matron, who seemed a little cranky. *Maybe it took a lot to look after so many girls.* I made a mental note not to get on the wrong side of her.

They showed us the essential rooms we might need today, and they would take us around to the rest a little later. I was happy to be in a dormitory with Robyn again, but a little sad they'd placed Rhonda in the nursery with the toddlers.

Rhonda would not stay in her room, however, preferring to sneak into ours and bunk with Robyn for the night. After many repeated nights of disturbance and continuous reprimand, the staff finally gave up and just left her there.

We arrived at a large room with a massive table tennis table dominating the middle. This day it was not used as intended but was covered in folded washing. Large piles of coloured hand-me-downs stacked ready for putting away. I supposed I'd be wearing some of those drab worn items soon enough.

I spied tall grey metal lockers, lined in a row along the wall like identical tin soldiers. Girls of various ages looked towards us as we entered the room.

'You can play in this area with the other children. I have things to do. Bye,' said our charge before leaving.

I felt like a fish out of water. No formal introductions made, just a brief statement thrown out into the room a few moments earlier. "Hi everyone we have three new girls. Please make them welcome." That was it, and we were left to handle this situation by ourselves.

It was like a silent film unwinding in my head, as I viewed the roomful of faces. I couldn't stop gulping air and I was swallowing hard. First day nerves were getting the better of me. I stood glued to the spot, as their eyes fixed in our direction.

Do I have a boogie hanging out my nose? Or perhaps my dress is tucked up at the back inside my undies. (I felt around there to make sure.) Nope that wasn't it.

Possibly my brain was just hell-bent on capturing the moment, but just when I thought they would never stop gawking at me, they turned away and continued with their own intention.

With no adults around, I watched their antics, this time at a normal speed. Without the attention on me, I could function as normal.

Gone were the gawks (much to my relief). The focus was now on each other. 'Hurry up! Let's do it,' said someone from the crowd.

'Keep a look out!' said another, to no one in particular.

Without hesitation, a horde of girls came forward and tossed the clean washing onto the floor in front of the lockers. Maybe to save themselves extra work they never touched the piles but instead used the scrunched-up ones waiting to be folded.

I watched in anticipation as the spectacle began.

Like a circus show they started to hoist themselves up onto a small table to the tops of the lockers. They stood like acrobatic stunt performers waiting for the crowd to cheer before jumping from their stage.

I screwed up my face and peeped through squinted eyes. I couldn't help thinking someone would surely get hurt from this bizarre behaviour. With every landing came a heavy thud. The clothes pile not really doing much.

I thought I'd just be watching the performance, but as it turned out, I ended up right in the thick of it.

'How about you new girls? Or are you too scared?' Came the challenge from one of the ring leaders.

Scared! She wouldn't know what real scared was. I'd lived my life through much more than this.

I stood there analysing the situation for a few minutes, while my peers waited for a response. I knew I wasn't getting out of this challenge without some fallout.

My brain was on alarm mode as it processed the possible scenarios. Maybe she was right, and I was scared. I hesitated just a little.

'Scared of what?' I used my tough smart-arse persona. The one I used to protect me from people hazards.

This tactic would usually bide me a little time to think as this was an unexpected response.

Trying to guess their expectation, I decided it could be some kind of initiation. But I couldn't be sure.

I surveyed the area and weighed up the risk. Lots of girls had jumped before me. I was not an agile type and my athletic abilities were nil. But I decided right there and then that I'd show them not to underestimate me. I was strong, smart and could do everything as good as them.

There were girls at the door popping their heads out every now and again to check if Matron or any of her army were about. I figured they had me covered. (I didn't want to get into strife.)

'Let's do it,' I said, ready to go.

My young heart was pounding from adrenaline. Slipping off my lace ups and socks (as I'd seen the others do), I got ready.

I went through the steps in my head. *First, I need to scramble onto the table. I am small and not a climber, so this is going to be quite an effort.* I placed my body over the table and my sisters came to help push me up on top.

Next, I need to scale the locker. Standing up, I placed two hands on the top. *This is easy,* I told myself repeatedly. With my foot now on the cool metal, I gripped my toes to the vertical wall. My other foot followed as I walked and tried to stay balanced. My arms extended across the top. One more shuffle and I was there.

I want to shout, *I'm not scared, see. I can do it just as well as you,* but I froze up and I had not looked down as yet.

Shaking, I rose slowly, holding on to the wall for stability. And as I turned hesitantly, a sea of cheeky faces stared up at me. They waited and it was how I imagined a rock star felt as he entered the stage. But I was not performing a song or striking an instrument. I was about to jump— maybe to my death! Perhaps if I closed my eyes, I could go through with this. But I knew this was stupid. If I closed my eyes I would surely die. How could I possibly put an end to this ridiculous dare.

Splat! I did it. How I got there was not clear in my mind, but I landed on my feet on a pile of clothes. And I breathed, for I escaped without incident, and for that I was thankful.

My brain was still catching up with my body, as I staggered towards my belongings. My sisters waited there. I saw them and I was grateful that I did not die.

'Quick! Someone is coming!' whispered the girls guarding the door. Panicked, I struggled to slip on my footwear. Many girls gathered up articles of clothing from the floor (well-practised perhaps) in a hurried frenzy.

No sooner had the shorts and tees been collected and the girls composed, than she entered the room.

I could tell Miss Doreen was a favourite. With her softly spoken voice, I was instantly calmed. The adrenaline rush had made it impossible for me to be able to tie my laces, my fingers trembled so much.

'Here, let me tie up your laces. I've just come down to check on you. Welcome to Kew, your new home,' she added as she smiled at me and my sisters too. 'Dinner is not far away.'

'Please Miss, can we go outside. Just for a little while. Plll..eee..se can we? We won't be long. We'll come in soon. Plll..eee..se.'

I didn't know the girls that were harping on, but it worked, and Miss Doreen let us go. 'Don't be long though, as it's nearly time to eat.'

My sisters and I didn't know where to go, so we followed the rest. It was the first time today that I'd been able to run free. Being in transition meant hours hanging out with adults. Now I could enjoy some fresh air, a run on the grass, and a dig in that sandpit.

But we forgot about dinner until the call from Matron, her voice grating the air like chalk across a blackboard. Fear replaced my joy at freedom.

A dominant authoritative figure, she seemed used to making the rules. My original opinion of her correct, it seemed.

It had been quite a day of emotion. Anxieties about leaving and arriving; escalations of adrenaline from happiness and risk taking. But today was going to end on a downward slide. I waited in the background for the fallout.

'Who said you could go outside?' she barked at us. 'You're all in trouble for not being washed up ready for your dinner.'

I tried to hide behind one of the girls. Matron's yelling was not a very nice experience on my first day. I was terrified at what was to come.

'Get inside and line up,' she bellowed! 'You know the rules and you all chose to ignore them. Now you will be punished.'

The pack crossed the grass in silence, each of us dealing with our own thoughts as to our predicament. It seemed like only seconds before we arrived back at our starting point. The table tennis table, still littered with garments, looked somehow smaller now the room was less crowded.

We shuffled in as she barked, 'Line up!'

Sweat rolled down my brow as I stuttered my objection. 'W… we didn't know the rules.' I was of course referring to my sisters alongside me.

'Get in line.' She pointed a gnarled finger in the right direction, ignoring my plea. I moved to line up behind Robyn. She now spoke up and gave it another go. (She wasn't one to usually take punishment quietly either.) Robyn insisted Matron show mercy as this was our first day and we didn't know the routine.

'Palms out,' she ordered, as Robyn's excuse fell on deaf ears.

We all stood there like battered soldiers. Our heads hung in sorrow but our hearts brave and trusting. Arms held out in front, with our palms facing upwards as she struck us on each hand with a hard plastic sandal.

It was not a light strike but a force that left great welts as it made contact with my flesh. One by one, each of us took our punishment. The pain, too much for some, had them crying. But she would not see me do the same. I would not give her satisfaction.

To treat my sisters and myself like that on our first afternoon, summed her up completely for me and I kept away from her as much as possible.

I never forgave her.

***

THE EGG

After a few days in our new home, I decided that my judgement of the Matron was warranted, after another episode with my sister, Robyn.

Mealtimes were a disciplined organised affair. I was expected to eat everything given to me. After all, how would I like to be one of those starving children in the world.

So I was thankful to God for making it rain, and bringing out the sun. Just, I'd like to tell them I already knew about those starving children of the world. But I was afraid they would chastise me for answering back if I dared open my mouth.

Robyn was served an egg. We all were. My thankful praise to God today was for making chickens. I liked eating eggs whereas my sister could not eat them without vomiting.

Just the smell of an egg was enough to make her nauseous and cause her to dry retch. To say she was livid at being dished out an egg, was perhaps an understatement.

Sliding the plate towards the centre a little away from her, Robyn sat and crossed her arms in defiance and waited. I knew she would be in strife as I watched the staff hovering like seagulls as I ate my fill with eyes cast forward.

It didn't take long for Matron to notice. Like a snake, she appeared to know just when to turn up and strike her poison venom. She spat it out at Robyn. 'Why haven't you eaten that egg on your plate? You will eat it. It's good for you!'

Robyn was ready for the venomous attack and stated confidently, 'I'm not eating that muck!'

I was flabbergasted at her spunk and it took great willpower not to laugh out aloud. I tried to distract my mind but nearly burst into a giggling fit when I looked over at Rhonda biting her lip and looking ready to burst.

I didn't dare look at either of them for fear of giggling and being punished. I waited with my head down, now listening to the argument. I knew for sure who would win this altercation and it certainly wouldn't be Matron.

'You'll sit there, until you do then!' The snake hissed.

'I can't eat eggs they make me sick,' Robyn said, screwing up her nose at the thought.

'Rubbish!' Matron seethed, standing over her in a power stance to bully her into compliance.

We were dismissed and cleaning up as Robyn sat there in disgrace. Her egg now stone cold and untouched. Her determination no match for Matron. Even the threat of extra punishment had no effect on the outcome. And Matron reluctantly had to admit defeat.

***

AN ARMY TANK

The story of Christ's birth began to circulate, and I knew Christmas was near.

My mother and dog were still missing from my life and no family members had visited. My feelings of sadness escalated at the realisation that I'd be without them at this special time of the year.

As I climbed from the bus in a scurry of children, I didn't know that today I was going to a Christmas party at Puckapunyal Army Training Base, only twenty minutes from the Highlands of my earlier years.

I huddled with my pack, shivering as I acclimatised to the sudden changes in temperature up here in the bush. Waiting for instructions, we practised our clap hands techniques.

The day was overcast with patches of rain. I ran on the spot, trying to warm up. The bush was still quite cool for this time of the year. The rain overnight had dampened the undergrowth of eucalyptus leaves and bark, giving the area a pine-scented fragrance.

I took a deep breath and savoured the aroma, its familiar smell a reminder of the past, of days spent in grass pastures, ice cold rivers and Christmas gumtree forests.

Miss Doreen and Miss Mary gathered us into a small group and marched us off to see the attractions. The rest of the kids headed in the opposite direction.

I went to watch the soldiers demonstrating the obstacle courses. People were zigzagging around me and it was really a bit hard trying to see everything.

Waiting in long lines was annoying and took forever. I waited until I really needed cordial before joining the queue. My mouth was so dry, I thought my lips would crack.

I joined in the organised activities and races. I wasn't very good at the races though, especially when I had a sack lifted up nearly to my armpits. The volunteers were very nice, however, and cheered me on.

Later on, I rode in an army tank. It was a massive muscle machine and I had to be lifted up to get inside.

I'm not much taller than the track belt wheels that made the line patterns in the dirt. The volunteers helped me get aboard through the circle flip top lid into the machine where the soldiers were. And I got to see all the gadgets in its innards. I didn't understand anything about war. It was the era of the Vietnam war, but I knew nothing about that. I was busy fighting my own.

Five minutes later, I was driven in the mud and I got to look outside through a peephole. I could only do this as a helpful soldier lifted me up. I couldn't imagine them shooting anyone as they were really lovely. I had a really good time.

All too soon it was over. Time to get a hoist out and give someone else an army tank experience.

I happily sat around and waited for the bus that would take me home. When we finally headed for home I sat and reflected. Today I was happier than I had been for ages.

***

HOLIDAY PEOPLE

A few days later they sent me away. No-one told me I was going on holidays for the summer, but here I was being escorted out the door with strangers I'd never met.

I was the first of my siblings to leave and my sisters were still in the building, but I did not get a chance to talk to them before I left.

I was anxious before I even got into their car. I did not want to leave without my sisters. We were inseparable and terror engulfed me that I might never see them again.

Maybe I would lose them all. My mother, my dog and now my sisters. I didn't want to be alone— by myself. I had been brave for so long and now I was really struggling to keep from crying.

The strangers talked to me in soft caring voices from the front seat. I had been shut in the back with their daughter Jane. I watched her as she looked me up and down. I could tell that she was privileged by her nice clothes. I was in one of my new dresses from Allambie. I had worn it often since I arrived in the home and it felt too familiar. My little suitcase had been put into the boot, but I didn't see it until I arrived at my accommodation.

I was right that they were privileged. I should've been grateful that they had invited me to stay in their modern two storey by the ocean.

It was afternoon and I was there to play with Jane, as she was an only child. *Jane must get lonely.* Suddenly I felt sorry for her, as I had two sisters and a mansion of girls to play with. So, I thought that maybe I was privileged, and she wasn't after all.

But then she seemed nasty to me and wouldn't share any of her rich toys. Everything I chose she was ready to take from me. We were not playing nicely together and so I decided to watch T.V. downstairs with her parents. But then she was cranky because I wouldn't play, and they were spending time with me.

I tried really hard to talk with her, but she was spoilt and privileged, and I, felt poor and not worthy. Her parents made me welcome, so I was happy to be near them today. I stayed the night and slept well in a house with loving parents and a clean orderly space.

I made some progress with Jane the next morning and she wanted to engage with me. Jane's mum took us out to the beach. It was just out the back gate and I thought I was going to stay here for a while and enjoy a seaside holiday.

The waves sounded familiar like when I had been paddling with Skippy. Only these were small waves as there was no wind and the sun shone so brightly today. I was in a happy space again. I missed the sea. 'Hello sea,' I whispered as I looked out into its magic aqua liquid.

Jane's dad stayed at the house. He'd smiled at me and said he'd get things ready for me. *He is a wonderful man.* I had never met a man who was so kind to everyone. So, I smiled back.

We were all going water skiing. I couldn't believe that I was going too. This would be my first time water skiing. Actually, this would be my first time in a motorboat too.

Jane talked to me and we started to tell secrets until her dad was ready to take us. Everyone was happy for a short while.

Aboard the boat, the engine gave a splutter and then roared to life. It was very noisy, and I blocked my ears at the sound. Jane showed me what the propeller was doing to the water and I watched it stirring up the gentle waves that had been lapping at the sides of the boat. It was all foam and bubbles, like Wizz Fizz powder swirling in water.

'Hold on tight!' Jane's father shouted over the noise. He didn't need to tell me. I'd already gripped the side of the vessel, a little frightened of all the noise. We hadn't travelled far, just out in the bay enough to get a good ski up, when he cut the motor.

I'd been given a life jacket to wear which made me feel like part of the gang. I liked being kitted out the same as the rest of the family.

'You can be first,' he said to me. 'I will show you.'

But Jane screeched and cried and threw the biggest tantrum I'd ever seen. *How embarrassing.* Did she know how ridiculous she was. What was wrong with her?

'I want to be first. It's not fair. Dad, I'm going first, not her!'

So, she went first and I watched. I didn't really mind, after all, she might show me how it was done.

But I never got a turn because I was not feeling well. Perhaps when I mentioned it, it was a little too obvious and they decided to end it there. Jane was back on the boat and we were off like lightning.

I was shattered as it was my turn and I wanted to have my first ever ski. But it was never going to happen because I was not feeling well. I was so disappointed but it was hard to concentrate as I was also a little lightheaded.

My life jacket was cast aside as I was shown the back gate. I felt like I was going to be sick and the world swirled around me like I had just jumped off the merry-go-round at the park. Thank goodness it was a short way to the house. Jane and her mother followed me with worried expressions on their pretty faces.

But now it was like an out of body experience. All picture, with the sound turned way down. I was still functioning, but I did not listen to them. I just needed to lie down.

I managed to climb the stairs into the bedroom and flopped down on top of the quilt, curled myself into the foetal position and closed my eyes.

But I could still hear them somewhere in my half-conscious state as they stood over me trying to communicate. 'Are you okay? What's the matter, Linda?

I wavered on the edge and tried not to fall into the void. I was not sure what was going on. I was feeling sick but managed to quiver.

'Jane is so mean to me. I wanna go home.' I cried soft tears and sniffed as snot started to run from my nose.

And it was the truth. *I just wanna go home.* But I was taken back to Blackhall. Blackhall my home for now. *Maybe forever.* Because I didn't know where home was anymore.

Robyn had left not long after me and had gone to stay in Phillip Island. And Rhonda was gone too, but Miss Mary didn't know where. So, I was sad that they were gone but I hoped they got to water ski and play at the sea like me. Maybe they would have a nice girl who took it in turns and didn't scream all day.

I was not alone, however. There were still girls here to play with, so I was not lonely, and I made the most of it.

Two days later Rhonda returned to keep me company and I hugged her and told her I was happy to see her. She said she had been with a mum and a dad and a little boy. It seemed, just like me, she wasn't having fun. She got scared and wet the bed more than once. The lady wasn't happy and really told her off. Rhonda got nervous and the lady felt bad, giving Rhonda glass beads out of her collection because she was sorry. It didn't make Rhonda feel any better, so Rhonda came home and now she was ill from a urine infection. Poor Rhonda, I felt bad for her. Holidays with strangers really weren't fun.

We now had each other so were happy to holiday at the mansion. We wondered if Robyn would ever join us again as she stayed away till it was nearly time to start school again.

Robyn couldn't wait to gloat about her fantastic beach adventure in Phillip Island. She told me she wanted to stay forever with Arthur and Martha. They had no children and doted on her all day. She could have whatever she wanted, and they were never too busy to spend time with her.

I felt happy as Robyn was always looking after us, and now someone had been looking after her. I was sorry she couldn't stay with her holiday people for longer.

***

MOTHER VISITS

Mother came to visit and I was thankful she hadn't forgotten me. I wanted to ask her many questions but she brought Grandma with her, which seemed very strange to me as Grandma was never in Victoria.

The Matron showed us to a large room I had not been in before. It looked like a sitting room as it had lots of comfortable old chairs to sit on. The type that only mansions were big enough to hold and only special visitors got to sit in.

Mother was thin and didn't talk very fast. I thought she still looked sick, but I wasn't sure why I thought this. My grandmother was behaving herself today and acting like she was a lady, instead of a hillbilly.

I had never before seen my grandmother dressed so nicely and being so polite. I thought perhaps my real grandmother had died and this was her twin sister. But then as she spoke, I realised she was still my family member, because no-one can talk that drool.

We had a nice catch up, however and Rhonda sat right up next to Mother, while Robyn and I sat opposite. I didn't want to sit too close as I wanted to look at her and make my own judgments. And I wasn't sure about Robyn as she wasn't good at showing her soft side.

Mother said she was sorry we were here without her, but she'd been terribly sick. I looked at her and believed her as she didn't look too healthy today.

Grandma butted in, 'Been in hospital for weeks. Darn near killed her with that treatment. Bloody doctors.'

I didn't know what she was on about, but she was already grating on my nerves.

I stayed quiet as I didn't want to feed her conversation. Mother continued and I was relieved. 'Yes, it's been terrible, but I'm on the mend. Mum can't take you home yet. They won't let me. Not until I have a proper home and an income to keep you. I'm so sorry. I am trying.'

I could tell she was sorry because she had tears in her eyes. And I went to hug her as I knew she was sorry. And I loved her. Robyn came over and joined us as we asked her a hundred questions. And Grandma was still ranting and making conversation on and off. None of us were listening to her though, as Mother held our attention.

I asked her about Skippy and she told me he was fine. I didn't need to worry as Bill was taking good care of him. I was relieved that Skippy was still alive, and Bill was looking after him. The only thing I didn't believe was that he was fine. I was certain he would be missing me and my sisters. So, I was still not happy for Skippy and I told Mother to make sure she told him I was coming home soon.

***

A MOVE TO KARDINIA

Early in March, we were moved to Geelong to be close to Mother. The Children's home was down on Riverview Terrace by the Barwon. I was not happy to be leaving the mansion in Kew. I wasn't sure about my siblings as they hadn't said much to me about it. Perhaps they were happy to be closer to Mother, so Kardinia would be sufficient for them. For me it was an old building but not on the same scale of grandeur as my beloved Blackhall.

On my arrival, I was taken into a small room and given pencils to colour in religious pictures.

We had brought with us a small boy to reunite with his sisters that lived here. While we waited, they took him to sort out what he needed. That was okay with me. He was a baby and didn't know any better. I thought the little baby boy was cute and it made me happy to know he would see his sisters again.

The first room at the top of the staircase had beds, lined up side by side and copied on the opposite wall. My bed wasn't far from the window so I could lie on it and see out onto the veranda through the glass.

Robyn bunked in with me as usual, and Rhonda again bunked in with the young one. This time she told me she was happy to stay and not worried about being separated from us.

Shady trees surrounded an old garden to play in. We didn't play that much, though, as we always kept busy. There weren't many hours left after I walked to and from school, and there were always chores to do.

Rhonda's favourite pastime was reading, and she spent a lot of time in the little library on the first floor.

Robyn made friends and busied herself most days just enjoying some friendship time. She was not so interested in having to mother Rhonda or me anymore.

I was healing, left to fade into the background of my new surroundings and just live. I didn't want drama or anger; I just wanted peace. Life was exhausting and I was tired.

Miss Jane was my favourite and always so kind to me. I could tell her all my worries and she listened. She was the kindest person I knew.

In her spare time, she had been sewing a toy clown and asked me if I'd like to keep it. I was surprised but very happy that she thought I would love him. I said, 'Yes please, I will look after him.' And she smiled back at me.

I liked to go to kids' club at the Salvation Army and church on Sundays. At least it was upbeat and everyone was happy to see you. So, my life was busy, and I was growing up fast.

Mother came to visit and sometimes my sisters and I were allowed access visits at the weekend. She still didn't have a home yet, so we were house guests of Bill's.

Bill was my mother's saviour and I liked him a lot. He was like my grandfather. No that wasn't correct. He was better than them, as I had never seen my grandfathers. Either of them. One lived in England and I'm not even sure if he was alive anymore. The other one no-one ever really spoke about, but I just knew he'd be a bad man.

Bill had a round kindly face, that always held a smile. He was strong because I'd seen his muscles, and Mother told me he liked to box.

Bill had a gym where he trained other people to be strong like him. 'It's on the hill not far away,' my mother said, 'but I'm too busy to show you.' So I figured, it was probably not a place for little girls.

'I have something new to tell you girls,' Mother said one day when we were out on our visit. My name is Joan and I am no longer May. I have been baptised with the Holy Spirit and now I am born again.'

It confused me, but I didn't need to worry as I never called her May anyhow. She was just Mother to me.

She took me to her new church. It was very different from the Salvation Army where I had been attending. There were no tambourines and trumpets playing hymns. Instead there was a rock and roll band, with drums, guitars and lead singers.

Everyone praised the Lord and then they talked in tongues. It sounded like Rhonda when she'd made up strange words and pretended she could talk another language. It was fascinating and a bit strange.

And one night during the service I was Baptised, but I was still Linda even though I was born again.

***

DISEASE AND ISOLATION

My sisters were sick. Matron told me I couldn't see them for a long time.

I liked this Matron in Kardinia even though she was the sister of the one in Kew. She was not the same. This Matron was chubby and cute. She greeted me with a lovely smile and always had time to talk to me. She was very kind and I liked her a lot.

My sisters along with another girl had Hepatitis A. 'It is very contagious. They must be isolated for many weeks,' the staff told us.

They shut them in a small room across from the foot of the stairs. As I ambulated the stairs in the morning, I was drawn to the door that held my sisters captive.

I thought they would die, and I wanted to be inside with them and wished I had hepatitis A as well. If they left me alone in the world, I would be lonely and surely die of a broken heart.

It was like solitary confinement. They couldn't escape and no one could enter without authority. I saw ladies that nursed them or staff that fed them allowed behind that door, and the doctor entered every now and again.

But I could not see them, and they could not see me. I was alone again, and time went so slowly.

Robyn perhaps was the sickest as she ate very little food. She was already a skinny stick figure and a fussy eater. The medical staff talked about her gaunt appearance to my mother, and she too was worried.

Uneaten portions created problems for Robyn as she was chastised severely. To save herself from the constant nagging, she took to hiding her leftovers in behind the cupboard. Her deception at fooling the staff and stopping their complaints eventually was exposed.

A hive of activity went on around the isolation room and I would only get snippets of information. They splashed disinfectant around and the smell made me dry retch as I passed by trying to sneak a little peek at my sisters.

"It's putrid, makes you sick, disgusting," were words being used as people scurried out. I was not just inquisitive, I'd heard that dead bodies stunk and worried that someone had finally died and they were cleaning up the decaying body parts.

The door was shut when I tried to look inside. I was ushered away and told not to hang around near the stairs. It was too much, and I ran off outside to be alone and wait. I was expecting bad news, so it was an anxious time.

When no-one came to find me, I thought maybe it was Helen who had died. And I thought this was terrible but then I thought better that it was Helen than my two sisters.

My mother arrived to pick me up, so they escorted me back inside and I asked her if anyone had died in that isolation room.

She laughed. 'What makes you think that?' she says. I told her my story as we headed out to her car. (An old Holden station wagon of white and maroon.) Then she told me about the mouldy rotten food, which made me laughed. It was just like Robyn to do that, and I was certain her roommates would never dare dob her in, or they would have what for.

***

HOME TO MOTHER

In September 1971, I was granted home release.

I had been living in care for eleven long months, but today I was going home to my mother. Leaving my sisters behind was terrible. 'They are still sick, but they're getting better everyday,' my mother said.

It didn't make me feel any better. Adults always lied, so how would I know if she was being truthful.

I only had her word that they'd be home soon.

The days dragged on slowly and I missed them terribly. As soon as they were allowed visitors, Mother and I went to keep them company.

I liked that I could still visit Kardinia and catch up with people I knew. It made the adjustment that little bit easier. I ran to find Miss Jane to tell her I was doing well and hoped she was too.

Mother was truly reborn, for my mother was different somehow. May's life had shattered and defeated her. I thought that perhaps May had died in the hospital during her treatment. Maybe she'd been electrocuted when they had wired her up with electrodes and pushed the button.

Joan was different from May— in a good way. More sensible, more stable, calm, and even I thought smarter. Yes, Joan was smarter.

Living with other children in a shared home taught me a lot about life. It was an experience I didn't totally dislike. I learnt to share, to care and to be independent. Now that I was home with Mother, it felt strange. Like she was an old friend instead of family.

I didn't know if I liked the quiet. I wasn't used to the silence in my new environment. I was bored, so Mother took me shopping and out to visit Skippy at Bill's to break the monotony.

My new home was in a block of commission flats at Coxon Parade. They were four little homes stacked together. Our flat was upstairs on the left.

Climbing its external staircase was quite a workout as it was very high. I stood standing on the little top landing and looked at the view of the houses and street below.

The parking bays for the cars were just outside the fence in the front. Being upstairs meant I could keep a lookout from my bedroom window and know who was or wasn't home. *I'm going to like it here. If only my sisters could hurry and join me, that would make it perfect.*

PART SIX:
THE FLATS

A man named Neckers came to visit me and Mother. He was tall and friendly with an accent. I liked him because he would drink cups of tea with us while listening to our stories. He was such a good listener and was so friendly that whenever Mother said he was coming, I looked forward to it with excitement.

By the time my sisters arrived home a month later, Mr Neckers was slowing his visits down and they only met him a couple of times.

And by the time he'd faded from our lives, I'd moved on as well.

Mother still attended church and they all pitched in to help with the furniture for our flat. The most memorable for me were the airplane chairs that sat in our lounge room. Someone had recovered them in modern green floral seventies material on a white background.

I found the inbuilt ashtray embedded into one of the arms a fascinating feature. Mother found it handy to fill up while she watched television.

Joan was a heavier smoker than May had been. Perhaps Joan had more money than May. Neither of them, however, had ever learned to do the draw back.

I got used to the smoke as it was just part of Joan. Besides I thought it was good when she ran out, as she would send us to the milkbar up on Church Street.

'Whoever goes can have some money to spend,' she'd say.

'I'll go,' I'd shout.

'I'll go too,' said Rhonda.

'You two are not getting all the money, gutses,' Robyn would say with her usual charming manners. We'd all have to go.

I loved standing in front of the lolly counter choosing my favourites. Sometimes it was a Wizz Fizz or Choo-Choo-Bar; candy necklace on elastic or a packet of Fags. I always felt like a tough girl with a candy fag in my mouth. I would practise the drawback and pretend to blow it out all over my sisters. And then I would suck the end with the red flame bit coloured on the end and pretend I burned my tongue.

But sometimes it was just a big bag of mixed lollies. At four and five lollies for one cent, there were always plenty to share.

***

GOODBYE BELOVED SKIPPY

I wanted Skippy home with us, but Mother said no, it was impossible to have him here at the flats.

I was cross as I couldn't see why not. I could take him for a walk to Church Street to get the smokes, and he could sleep inside. He'd been in the station wagon in the Kimberly and behaved himself perfectly. I didn't see why he had to live at Bill's.

Bill's was nice but that backyard of his was more like a junkyard. Full of bits and pieces of second-hand rubbish. Bill like to repair things but had trouble storing it appropriately. Junk was stacked up in the corners of his residential block; televisions, electrical goods, gym equipment, mechanical odds and sods and an array of other hard scrap, littered the space.

I felt sorry for Skip living in a messed-up backyard for a good part of his day. The high wooden fence meant he couldn't see people. Skippy loved people and without human contacts, he would be lonely and bark all day.

I really wanted to have him with me, but I couldn't, and it made me sad. I'm sure that in my sleep I heard his barks of misery to come and rescue him.

The neighbours complained, and he got move to the front where the brick fence was too low and he started bothering the postman. He was a nice postie, though, and brought him a dog biscuit every day. Bill said it was okay now and Skip was being good.

Mother came home not long after that and told me Skip was gone.

'What do you mean? I asked her.

'He bit the postman and he's been put to sleep.'

I didn't believe her, and I told her he liked the postie. She said it was a different one. I'd already started bawling as she tried to explain. I didn't want to hear her explanation. I hated them— her and Bill— they'd killed Skippy and I would never forgive them for that.

Mother moved on and bought a new dog; a small one she could hide in a flat. A dog that no one would complain about. I mourned Skippy like I'd mourned my doll Pamela. And the sudden end to his life cut into me like blade slicing my heart. It truly was that painful.

***

THE FLATS

The new puppy was very cute with his freckled belly and shaggy white and brown coat. His name was Danny, but my family fondly called him Danny Dog. He slept in a white cane baby bassinette. Every day my sisters and I took turns to walk him around downstairs.

At first, we tried to hide him, so no-one would tell on us for having a puppy inside our home, but many of our neighbours owned animals anyhow. I could see cats slinking in behind doors and some were carrying toy breeds under their arms. Everyone had the same idea. So, we were all happy for the secret to be between us.

I was quite happy here in our two-storey cement flat with a rendered exterior painted a yellow cream, the same as the others beside it. The staircase was on the outside like a cement fire escape.

The interior had been painted too many times, the skirting was too dark, and the walls got damp in the winter. But it was home and I felt safe and happy at last.

Rich families didn't live here, but I felt richer than I ever had. And living upstairs gave me a great vantage point to watch whatever was going on outside.

Out of my bedroom window, I could see the other houses in the parade. And if I wound it out, I could speak to Mother in the car park, to tell her to wait, when I was not quite ready to go.

Our kitchen faced down the back of the block towards the boundary fence.

I liked looking out into the back while doing the dishes. Up here I could see everyone on their laundry wash day.

I usually dried the dishes, as Robyn loved to wash. I liked to wash too, but Robyn loved being bossy and never let me. She didn't let Rhonda either.

We rarely challenged her because the consequences were just too great. She'd get her claws out or rip out handfuls of hair from our scalps. Challenge her and all hell broke loose.

Joan had more money than May ever had. I liked living with her, as it was the first time in my life I could buy fashion clothing. Joan put them on lay-by until she paid them off.

Now that I was pre-pubescent, it was all about the clothes. One day I got my first pair of purple cord Levi's. I thought I was the luckiest 10-year-old in the world.

Mother liked us to look nice, so she'd buy us furry jackets with cow hide design, and tartan skirts attached to white singlet tops. She knitted us jumpers and crocheted ponchos. She sewed us floral long dresses and ironed on heart patches to decorate our jeans.

Nothing was out of bounds. There was three of everything. Treads, Volleys, and gym boots. Lacy knee-high socks for going out and rainbow toe socks for fun. I've never owned so much fashion.

One of my Aunts was getting married, so Joan made us matching smocked frocks that had taken her weeks. Pretty white nylon with red smocking on the bodice, with a strap that tied at the back in a bow. I felt like a princess.

We only had two bookend beds in our room when we first arrived, so Rhonda bunked up with Mum or Robyn. But that's okay, no-one seemed to mind.

Dad never paid any money, even though Mum was always trying to make him. And he never came to visit even when we were little. The only time we spent with him was when mother took us on a road trip to visit him.

She took us to Deniliquin on the way to the wedding. Father took us shopping in the department store with the massive windows under the wide Victorian verandas. It'd been in the same place for years. I got to choose an outfit. It was a lovely brown and cream paisley patterned slack suit that suited my green eyes and auburn hair.

Last time we visited him, he bought me a watch. I'd never owned a watch before, so I was grateful. But truthfully, I would have loved a pretty bracelet instead.

I think he was lucky our mother took us to visit him as he really didn't deserve it. He was my dad though. The only one I would ever have, though he was a funny friendly man with his little ditties and inappropriate jokes.

He talked of old England and the family he'd left behind. No-one else had stolen his heart again. He told me he still loved my mother. *But*, I thought, *you have a strange way of showing it.*

Father shouted us raspberry sodas while he drank beer. In the pub, he showed us off like his life prize. Everyone knew him as he'd been coming here for years. He lived at the pub in a room up on the balcony. He took us upstairs and we played there until Mother came back and took us out to Grandma's.

The wedding was lovely, and we got to see family that we hadn't seen for ages. Everyone wanted to see how we were now after being away so long. I told them I was fine and went off to play. I didn't want their sympathy.

Grandma was losing her farm. Something went wrong and she would be moving to Victoria with Martha, but they didn't tell me anything anymore. I figured I was allowed to be sad. Sad I'd never go to the farm again. I'd miss that muddy looking river and those majestic trees.

***

BEST FRIENDS FOR EVER

I met a new friend. Actually, she met me as I rounded the corner from my flat to the grassed yard. She'd already met my sisters when I'd arrived. A beauty with thick long brunette curls that bobbed around as she moved her head. Her eyes with irises the colour of faded Lapis Lazuli blue. Her long black lashes highlighted their beauty. And her perfectly shaped lips turned into a massive smile as she spotted me. It was instant love for the two of us. And we would be best friends forever.

Suzanne became family and we were inseparable. If she didn't visit me, then I would visit her. She stayed over at nights if her mum or mine went out. Or I'd stay at hers and help babysit her little brother. There was hardly a day went by that I was not with her. And she brightened my life like no-one else had.

It was never the same without her, especially on outings or holidays. Bill had organised the vehicle for Mother. Even though its maroon and white deco was faded, it still ran well and had recently transported us all the way to Deniliquin and back. She was proud of it and parked it down in the little parking bays, just out the front of our flat. Its wide vinyl bench seats were perfect for Rhonda and me. And there was still plenty of room for Danny's baby bassinette in the back. Robyn, of course, was the only one allowed on the front bench with Mother, unless she was somehow not aboard. And then it was whoever was first to claim. It was like the dishes— it wasn't worth the fight.

It could fit six people easily. No-one wore seatbelts in those days, so any extra passengers just squished up together.

With Robyn, everything she wanted she got because she made sure it went that way. She was insecure as we all were but her frustration at being poor perhaps affected her more.

'I'm not being seen in that old rust bucket. How embarrassing,' she said to Mother.

'Don't be ridiculous, how else can you get to school,' Mother said.

But Robyn made Mother park around the corner a long way from the school gate. I was annoyed at how Robyn behaved. It didn't bother me if it was an old car. I was happy enough to be dropped close so as I didn't have to walk, but what I wanted wasn't even considered.

Eventually Mother gave up and stopped driving us altogether and we all walked to school, but that turned out great for me as Suzanne was allowed to come too.

Crossing Church Street's extremely busy traffic was challenging but we all got used to it. After all, we'd grown up walking in Melbourne. I actually enjoyed the walk up Pakington Street amongst the shops and businesses. And Suzanne and I loved to chat all the way, side by side, while my sisters strolled together at their own pace.

The Catholic kids love to tease us and we teased them back. 'Catholic wogs, sitting on logs, eating gizzards out of frogs.'

I didn't know who started the taunt, but they were always swearing and threatening us as well. Each of us giving cheek to one another. No one really getting out of hand. So I put it down to childhood banter and didn't take it to heart.

Ashby Primary was in Lawson Avenue, but we entered from Waratah Street. Like my schools in Melbourne, it was a lovely architectural masterpiece of Edwardian splendour. Its red brick exterior familiar and welcoming.

I loved this school and I was happy to go. My grade five teacher, Mr Saunders was an ace at sports. I hated sport and avoided it like the plague. But something was different about how I played sport in grade five. For the first time I didn't have to prove myself. I was allowed to play rounders or basketball out on the asphalt with my class and just enjoy it.

***

THE BIRD DOWNSTAIRS

Mrs Wren lived downstairs diagonal to us. She was more like a plover than a wren, though really. We'd just moved in recently and didn't know the pecking order. Mrs Wren, it turns out, was on the top.

'We need to do some washing. Come on. Downstairs and help. Grab the washing powder,' Mother said.

Boring. I didn't want to do laundry. By the way they were whining, neither did my sisters.

Joan didn't like *no* for an answer, so I reluctantly went hunting for the powder, while she scoured around for any other dirty items.

Five minutes later, we were all out the door and down the stairs.

As we entered the washroom with our basket of dirty clothes, the Plover arrived to join us. We saw her waddling towards us from her flat like a half-crazed moron flapping her wings in defence. 'What are you doing?'

Not a hello or some polite introduction, instead she pouted her lips and puffed up her cheeks, waiting for an explanation.

'I'm gonna do some washing. We've moved into number three.' Mother pointed in the direction of our upstairs windows. 'The girls are helping me.'

'Washing! You can't wash today!'

'Why isn't it working? I haven't loaded it yet,' Mother said a bit puzzled.

Who was this short bespectacled woman, blocking the doorway with her bulk?

Self-assured and arrogant, she enunciated her words slowly, 'I'm Mrs Wren. And it's my day to wash.'

I made my judgment of her straight away, instantly disliking her. I was sure she was used to bullying people around to get what she wanted.

'You don't own the laundry. I need to do some washing,' Mother said.

'That's the way it is. We take it in turns. Now please, if you don't mind? I have washing to do.' Mrs Wren pushed her way past us, and as we picked up our laundry items, she began running the water and ignoring us.

'You're so rude.' Joan sneered at our plover neighbour as we exited the room.

Mrs Wren paid us no more attention. She had gotten her way, and it seemed that was all that mattered to this old bird.

I wasn't impressed with Mrs Wren.

'She's an old bitch for treating us like that,' said Mother.

Later when Suzanne arrived for a play, I explained what the Plover had done earlier today. 'Let's get back at her. What d'you think, Rhonda?'

'Yeah, what a mean old bag,' she replied. Sue shook her head and the plan was hatched.

We'd take a piece Plover's underwear off the clothesline and show it to all our neighbours.

We agreed, it would be her girdle, with its little clips on the end of the straps, and its tight elastic panels to help pull in her bulging midriff. It was the ugliest piece of underwear we'd ever seen. And perfect fodder for embarrassing her.

It would be fun to show everyone old fat Plover's choice in underwear. We screwed up our noses at the thought of even handling it.

I snuck down sometime later and removed it successfully from the line. It was a nylon flesh-toned affair, which made it all the more ugly.

I held the girdle by one of its dangling suspender straps and raced it upstairs. Swinging it like a cowboy trying to lasso a Bronco, I chuckled to myself. 'Look what I've got,' I said with a smug look.

Rhonda and Suzanne were gobsmacked. 'She's done it!' They giggled.

I tried to say something, but instead burst into laughter. We all did. And the tears ran down our cheeks as we rolled around on the beds trying to contain ourselves. We'd teach her to mess with us.

Downstairs we carried that gut buster with confidence, knocking on the neighbourhood doors, politely asking the occupants if they knew who owned the girdle. Suzanne made sure it was held up so everyone could get a real good look at it. I stood as she blurted her practised lines, scanning the ground so as to not make eye contact. And with Rhonda nudging her elbow into me, it was sheer torture holding back the laughs.

No one lay claim to it of course, until we knocked on the Plover's door. 'Oh, hello, we found this girdle. Do you know who it belongs to?' I asked her.

Suzanne stepped forward and held it up just centimetres from her face.

'Oh, it's mine, thank you. It must have blown off the line. Good girls,' she said to us with gratitude in her voice.

Rhonda and I were holding in our giggles, ready to burst. I really needed to get away before I wet myself. Sue was so good at keeping a straight face while taking the piss out of people that I threatened to ruin it all.

We all ran off to release our laughter. Satisfied we'd payed her back with our girdle sequence.

***

THE CRAZY OLD LADY

Mother headed downstairs with the puppy. She wanted to reward him with a giant beef bone she'd bought him from the butcher's earlier. We followed her downstairs to play on the grass. 'Mind the puppy while I hang the washing on the line. Oh, and give him this,' she said, handing me a massive femur bone.

She plonked Danny on the grass and went to check on the washing.

I stared at the bone.

Was she for real? It was at least twice as big as the dog.

Danny got a whiff of it however and started barking. Scared I may be chastised for the noise, I placed it down beside him and watched his response.

Bounding towards it, he attacked it with sharp baby teeth. His tiny body draped over its surface. I was surprised and amused at Danny's enthusiasm as he ripped off tiny strips of meat.

He'd just got started when a peculiar old lady appeared from nowhere. Picking up the bone in one fowl swoop, she headed towards the large garbage can lined against the back fence. 'How disgusting, leaving bones lying around like that,' she muttered loudly to herself, walking straight past us all like she hadn't seen us. A slim woman dressed all in black with a white bun twisted tightly on her head. I hadn't seen her before and wondered where she lived. She had an air of arrogance and immediately had me intrigued.

'Hey! That's our dog's bone,' Joan shouted after the woman.

'It's in the rubbish now! Dirty old thing!' she answered turning slightly but continuing on her way.

Mother was fuming and sprouted off. 'How dare she, the cheek of some people!'

Retrieving the bone from the garbage, she made her way back towards our home at number three. Placing the bone on the top of our landing, she decided Danny Dog could continue eating it tomorrow.

***

MAKING FRIENDS

Joan started taking us to her newfound church group. We all joined in the service and the singalongs. It was almost like a rock band with guitars and drums and a couple of lead singers backing up the lyrics to the Christian hymns.

Mother began to make friends and take us to play with their children. She learned to talk in tongues along with the rest of the congregation. Joan seemed to have her life under control, something May never really had. But I wasn't sure what was really going on.

She had me hypnotised in an attempt to help me forget the abuse. I saw a charlatan that tried to rid me of bad vibes and auras or something of that nature. He was a whacked out looking guy, wearing therapeutic sandals with spikes. He asked me to lie down and relax, which was darn hard with a total stranger staring down at me and chanting stupid rubbish.

Maybe Joan thought I was possessed as I still complained of dizziness and a feeling of faintness every once in a while. Perhaps it made her feel better. Mother was still dabbling into the supernatural and visiting clairvoyants in an attempt to foresee the future. I wondered really what the hell she was doing? It really only made me feel worse. I did not protest even though I should've.

Mother made friends with a Croatian couple and their three young daughters. They were not church friends but new proprietors of Bill's Service Station.

We met up often and my sisters and I each had a little child to cuddle and look after. Our families enjoy regular picnics and outings at Eastern Beach.

On sunny days we'd arrive at Eastern Beach laden with picnic food— meats, cheeses and bread in particular. Also bottles of sweet cordial and flasks of coffee.

Eastern Beach was a favourite. Racing down the big Spanish staircase to the magnificent fountain half-way down, I'd pause to take in the spectacular views of the ocean. And then I'd be off again down the next flight and on to the dressing pavilion, where I'd strip along with the other five girls and throw on my bathers. Our mothers entered the room just as us kids were racing out.

'Be careful and watch the little ones. One each, remember. We'll be out in a minute.' They would both wave us off, confident we would be responsible. Which of course we were.

We never waited long for them but with a small child each to pair up, they knew we were the ideal babysitters.

The young ones liked the little cement pool with the fountain in the middle. It was safer for them and less crowded with teens, so we spent a lot of time there.

The adults, of course, enjoyed the deeper water of the sea baths. With its semi-circular platform boardwalk and a large diving board at the deep end, it was a great place to swim.

I applied zinc cream to my nose and across my cheeks, but that was the extent of my sun protection. (No sunscreens in those days). I certainly never wore a hat or covered up. I'd run in the sun with the rays tanning my fair skin. (If I was lucky.) With my auburn hair and green eyes, too much exposure sometimes meant blistered skin.

We'd get tired of swimming and climb the grassy slopes. At the top I'd lie down and squeal with delight as I rolled down the hill at full speed.

Soft green terraced lawns, watered and manicured, were just sheer luxury under my bare feet.

I'd sit with my family under big palms, peppercorns and cypresses that towered towards the sky, carefree and happier than I'd ever been in my life before. I loved my picnic under the shade with the people I loved.

Our families enjoyed many wonderful outings to St Helens Beach, Ripple Side, Fairy Park and the You Yangs at Little River.

Bill even let us stay in our old house in Ocean Grove, where I revisited the shores of my early childhood, and explored the beaches of Queenscliff, Point Lonsdale and Barwon Heads.

We lived on wog bread (as they called Vienna loaf), sliced mortadella, salami, and fish and chips.

Our holidays with Cathy and Andy were never without ice-creams— Dixie Cups, Drumsticks or Paddle Pops.

It truly was the best time of my life.

***

THE PIPES

Outside our boundary fence at the back was a scruffy parcel of land. On that council plot, high off the ground, sat large concrete wastewater pipes. Their presence was a beacon to us, just waiting to explore.

One day we decided it was time to get out there and have a really good look at them. We knew we'd never be allowed to climb them, so we were careful not to mention our intent to anyone. Especially our mums.

Slyly exiting out the front gate of Suzanne's block of flats (they faced Baxter Road), we raced quickly (so as not to be seen) onto the neighbouring land.

Stretching out before us was a great expanse of grassland, but we weren't interested in exploring any of it. Instead we were drawn to the massive pipeline.

It protruded from the earth, spanning the furrow that ran like a scar through the land. Its smooth grey cylinder walls looked like a great piece of play equipment, and we couldn't wait to get up there.

Our small physiques were dwarfed against its enormity. This made it quite a challenge to climb, but we didn't let that deter us at all.

We discovered we could reach it by standing on the earth where the pipe was protruding, and we were able to pull ourselves into the gutter that ran the length of the pipe.

One by one we helped each other climb in, until we were all perched in the trough. Sitting up there, we admired the view for ages. A feeling of immense pride filled me. How clever were we for finding such an awesome lair.

For the next few months, we visited the pipe on a regular basis. It was our secret and we did not tell.

Visiting every chance we got, we soon became bored with just running along inside the gutter, and began to heave our bodies up onto the top of the massive cylinder construction.

Being up so high was a little un-nerving at first but exciting at the same time.

To begin with, we crawled along the top on all fours like timid animals, but after a while our courage increased and stood upright to walk along them.

Each time we visited, we became a bit more brazen, until finally we could run along them without fear of falling. The lure of adventure started overruling our common sense.

In the dirt we found the drains that allowed us to enter inside the pipe. We jumped into them and walked with our legs splayed on either side of the wall. Dirty water trickled between our feet.

One day we walked all the way to the golf course in North Geelong. We recognised the area as we peeped through the slit in the drain. It amazed us that we had travelled so far under the city.

It seemed we were not the only occupants inside, as we heard something running around. The echoing noise of scratching and screeching amplified, as it bounced off the smooth curved walls inside the pipe.

'What was that!' Rhonda squealed.

'Probably rats,' said Robyn with an air of confidence I didn't think she really had.

'Rats. Yuck, I'm out of here.'

Rhonda turned and bolted and I was close behind. Everyone started squealing and running and we couldn't get out of there fast enough.

None of us saw any rats that day, but we never went again. Which I think was a good thing as we were possibly in danger of hurting ourselves on those drain water pipes.

**

SINGING STARS NEED
SOMEWHERE TO PRACTISE

Suzanne and I enjoyed dressing up in elaborate clothes. Like all little girls, we spent hours singing and dancing. During the summer months especially, we'd be on the grass out the back singing till one of us had to go inside.

We'd pretend to be rich and famous, singing to invisible people with hairbrushes for mics. We were talented; everyone would want to come and see our show. Or so we liked to believe.

Sometimes my sisters would join us but mostly it was Sue and me.

With all this singing and dancing, Mother decided to enrol us into a jazz and tap-dancing group. Maybe the finances dried up, as it was a short-lived exercise, though one which I really enjoyed.

She bought us black tap shoes with little loose taps nailed to the bottom of the leather soles.

I learnt to chant my steps as I tap danced in class. Shuffle hop behind, shuffle hop behind. Tap, tap, tap. Heel toe, heel toe, tap, tap, tap. It was so much fun.

Mother made our costumes, all three the same with silver fleck thread. We practised for months to perform on stage to The Lion Sleeps Tonight, my one and only highlight in entertainment.

As winter arrived, we were cold and needed somewhere to play. The laundry was perfect, and we sang and danced by the washing machine to keep warm. It was crowded but at least it was better than being in the cold.

But the old Plover locked us out— for what reason we never knew. So, this was war. We'd make her pay for her treatment of us. Who did that old Mrs Wren think she was? The laundry guard.

We would take the louvred glass from the window, and climb in through the little cavity. 'We'll have to be careful not to break any. Otherwise we will be found out, and then be in deep trouble,' I said to my bestie.

'Let's do it,' she said.

We found a few bricks that we stacked together to reach the glass. Climbing on the rickety pile, I tried to carefully pull out the slats. 'Aww they're sharp,' I said pulling my hand back.

'You pass them to me, and I'll lay them on the grass,' said Suzanne.

I tugged on them a little more, wriggling them slightly. 'That's better, I have one,' I said, as I turned to hand it to Suzanne. She placed it on the grass while I continued to work away at the rest of the window slats. Cautiously, I worked each one out of its groove and into the hands of my best friend.

Once we had them out, it enabled us to fit through the cavity. Grabbing our dress-ups and paraphernalia, we pushed them through the opening. Satisfied they were scattered somewhere inside, we now, one at a time, placed our hands on the sill and hoisted our bodies up off the ground and into the laundry.

'Hooray, we made it,' Sue said as she too landed in the cement trough beside me. We were happy to be inside out of the cold and it felt victorious to be such a rebel.

I had always had music in my life. When there was nothing else there was always Mother's records to play and dance to. And on any road trips we took as a family, we always sang.

I watched music shows like The Partridge Family and Young Talent Time, and at school I learnt songs from the broadcast on the crackled speakers in the classroom.

With plenty of material to sing, we'd play happily for hours until we'd tire of stardom and retired our voices for the day.

In revenge for locking us in, we unanimously decided that we would piss in the troughs.

We pulled up our costumes and downed our undies. Perched with our bums over the troughs, we fired.

Hot urine steamed up the cold cement as the sound of fizz filled our ears. And we threatened to fall inside on top of it from laughing so hard. 'That will teach her.' We giggled as we made ourselves decent again, threw the items back out on the lawn, and headed out through the window space.

'Let's go!' said Sue. 'Mum will kill me if she catches me.'

We placed the glass louvred panels back in like nothing had happened and went our separate ways.

***

A WITCH WITH SHERBETS

Suzanne lived on the ground floor in the first block of flats that face Baxter road. Her block had a staircase in the middle and an undercover breezeway in the centre, where we played with Barbies.

Her mother had recently bought her some lovely dolls with all the accessories. Beautiful knee-high boots, handbags and elaborate fashions. Her Barbies were high-class fashion models. Mine were the girl-next-door type.

She also owed a handsome masculine male doll by the name of Ken. I brought my Barbies over to date Ken, but he wasn't interested in the girl-next-door type. His focus was on the gorgeous fashion models. He was the typical egotistical type male.

Sue stripped her models and had them engaging in rude sex acts. *Just as well my Barbies aren't his type.* My ladies were well behaved and managed to keep their clothes on in his presence most of the time.

Suzanne owned a Skipper too, the young pre-teen doll, which was really cool. I loved playing Barbies with her. She always shared and I got to play with the latest things.

It was the middle of winter and the morning was freezing cold. It had been raining hard for a couple of hours. I didn't want to play upstairs with my sisters, so I raced over to Suzanne's to see if she was keen.

Her mother was busy, so we were sent outside into the breezeway to make our mess.

Sue retrieved her dolls from the broom cupboard, and we settled down to sit under the stairs to play. It was a little chilly, but we were happy to be together and hardly noticed.

As we sat on the cement floor, we spread the contents of the box over the floor and soon became engrossed in our game.

Suzanne and I started to dress her dolls, choosing articles of favourite clothing to adorn them with, and hunting for just the right accessories. Suzanne dressed Ken in his flared jeans and floral open-necked shirt, so he could parade around and show off his good dress sense.

We were laughing and having a lovely time, when the bottom flat door opened, and out walked old Mrs Lambert.

Her clothes were always black and drab, and today she had a raincoat over the top in the same colour to keep her dry from the rain. She clutched a shopping bag in one hand and an umbrella in the other. Mrs Lambert was perhaps the most peculiar person I think I had ever encountered. She was really quite looney. Sue and I were always a little scared of her.

We thought she must be a witch; why else was she always dressed in black flowing robes? I thought all she needed to complete her outfit was a pointed hat.

Maybe she was grieving and suffered dementia, but I was too young to know any of that.

'Hello, girls.' She addressed us in a pleasant soft voice.

Looking up from our position on the floor, we cautiously replied, 'Oh hello.'

She hardly ever spoke directly to us, so we were quite taken back. I stared at her, frozen to the spot. *What did she want?*

She rubbed her hands together. 'It's too cold for you little girls to be sitting on the concrete. I will grab you a blanket to sit on.'

Retrieving the key from her coat pocket, she placed her basket beside the front door, unlocked her flat and returned inside.

I wanted to say it was okay, that we'd be just fine, but she had disappeared and was already searching for something. So I continued my game, soon losing interested in what she was doing.

The witch returned moments later with a thick woollen blanket and fluffed it out beside us. 'There you go, darlings. Oh, and I have a lovely surprise for you. Here are some little sweets.' She smiled at us. 'You're such lovely girls.'

I was totally flabbergasted as she tipped a fist full of lemon sherbets onto the blanket, picked up her basket and descended the front steps. 'See you when I get home,' she called back. And she left. Her pointed laced shoes clip-clopped as she walked away down the street.

If I hadn't heard the echo of her shoes on the pavement, she had disappeared so quickly, I would have thought she'd flown away on her broom.

'Do you think those are poisonous lollies?' I said, staring at the lollies strewn on the blanket.

'You try one first,' Suzanne said to me.

'All right, but if I'm poisoned, you will have to go tell Mum.'

'Yeh, okay,' Sue said. Not too concerned.

I reached over, picked one up and turned it over a couple of times for inspection. I figured I'd be able to taste the poison if she'd laced them. If they were bitter, I'd just spit it out and I wouldn't swallow.

I gingerly licked a tiny portion of the yellow surface, its sharp taste heightening my alert senses, making me pause. No! This was not bitter. It was sour. And now it was sweet to taste.

Could this be poison? I processed it in my mind. *Maybe she'd added sugar to disguise the taste.* I wasn't sure. I decided to err on the side of caution and not eat it.

Sue popped one in her mouth. 'Mmm, they taste good.' Suzanne had already bitten into the sweet, and was curling the corner of her eye at the explosion of flavour from the sherbet centre.

I waited to see if I needed to run and get her mum. I really didn't like the prospect of seeing my best friend gasp her last breaths.

Off in my own thoughts, I was suddenly jolted back to the moment.

'Nope! I haven't died yet. They taste pretty normal,' she said. 'Let's share them up.'

Sharing the remainder, we ate them at our leisure, and continued on with our game.

Later in the morning, Mrs Lambert returned with her purchases and climbed the steps. I heard her coming and smiled as she approached us.

'Hello,' we chanted together.

I had never felt friendly towards her before, but I was thinking perhaps I had misread her and maybe she was really quite nice. *I would give her another chance.*

She just stood there glaring at us. 'What are you two children doing sitting on my blanket?' she said in a screeching voice.

We looked at each other in surprise. *What the hell was she on about? Was she joking?* 'You gave it to us to sit on,' I said. 'Don't you remember?'

'Get off!' she yelled.

We were trying to get out of her way as she dragged it from underneath us. Toys and accessories tumbled off the rug and scattered everywhere across the cement floor.

Like a gust of storm wind or a magic trick, whoosh and it was gone. Mrs Lambert disappeared with the blanket tucked under her arm, slamming her front door in a show of arrogance.

Suzanne and I gathered up our playthings in a hurry. I didn't want to hang around and I think Sue felt the same.

'See I told you she was a witch. She's evil,' I said. 'Let's hurry up in case she comes back.'

'Yes let's,' said Sue.

***

REFLECTION

Living in the flats was never boring. I was having so much fun and adventure. It felt good to finally be settled and have somewhere to call home. I had a best friend— something I'd never had before. Previously, I'd never stayed long enough anywhere to make one.

Mrs Wren didn't bother us anymore. We almost forgot she was living downstairs.

Old Mrs Lambert continued to waver between sane and totally barmy, singing hymns to the Lord at the top of her voice for all of us to hear. I was never far away, laughing at her silly antics or trying to get out of her way. She'd spend hours watering the Hydrangeas that grew in the garden beds, and waiting for an unexpected fool to target.

She'd hose them down in their cars as they stopped at the corner. Squirting them through their open window. Or soak any single man that dared to walk the paths to visit one of the unmarried females in the buildings. *(Doing the Lord's work on fornication,* I thought.) And it did them no good to confront a demented old woman, for she had no remorse. She'd just brush it off with a quote from the Bible.

One day, two fire trucks arrived on Baxter Road. Their sirens were screaming and their lights flashing. The building was on fire. Thick smoke could be seen billowing out of the windows. A crowd had gathered in earnest, ready to evacuate.

Imagine our surprise when old Mrs Lambert leant out. 'Oh sorry, I've just burnt my peas, dear.' She beamed a broad smile, totally unaware of the trauma she'd caused.

My siblings and I had dealt with a lot in our short lives. We'd had many sad times, bad times, and times that were just plain crazy, but now there was light. Life was getting better. I had seen a lot of bulldust. But I'd also met loads of lovely people and explored many exciting places and I learnt to blow that dust off.

I was 11 years old and I would soon be really into pop music, fashion and boys. But not before a couple more moves and more disruption. But that's all another story.

THE END

Acknowledgements:

Thank you to:

My family and friends who always believe and encourage me. Their love is dearly appreciated.

Editor, Serena Sandrin for her patience and expertise.
http://www.sandrinediting.com   storyeditor1@gmail.com

Author, Peter Edwards who inspired me to write and keep going.
www.allminestories.com

Photographer, Baz Landy for his fabulous photo image of the outback that adorns my book cover.
http://www.thelandy.com

And my talented son, Hugh Jeffreys for the cover design.
Hughjeffreys.com

LINDA PARKER

www.ingramcontent.com/pod-product-compliance
Lightning Source LLC
Chambersburg PA
CBHW072138090426
42739CB00013B/3216